Alí Na<u>kh</u>j

CW01511857

TOWARDS
WORLD ORDER

2004

Bahá'í
Publications
Australia

TOWARDS WORLD ORDER
1st Edition- 2005
© Copyright 2005 - Casa Editrice Bahá'í – Ariccia

This Edition – 2006

 Bahá'í
Publications
Australia

Cover design: Masoud Tahzib

ISBN 1 876322 93 4

Distributed by
Bahá'í Distribution Service
P.O. Box 300
Bundoora Vic 3083
Australia
Email: bds@bahai.org.au

Sixty young Bahá'ís from 24 countries in Europe gathered in Acuto for a week-long course on the study of various aspects of the World Order of Bahá'u'lláh. This course was arranged by the National Spiritual Assembly of Italy, in consultation with the Board of Counsellors in Europe.

The attached notes are transcripts of the six presentations made during the week. The reader will find some overlapping of issues in one or more of the talks. Such repetitions have not been eliminated in order to keep the text of the talks as presented to the class.

The questions asked and the answers given have been sorted according to the themes of the presentation each day and appear at the end of the text of each of the six talks.

The points raised in these notes are for the most part based on the Writings of our Faith, as I have understood them. Shoghi Effendi has warned the friends that the future will witness attacks on the Administrative Order. It is hoped that the themes presented and the conclusions drawn in these notes will assist the participants of this course to defend the Cause against these attacks in the days to come.

Alí Nakhjavání

CONTENTS

In order to place this subject in its proper context it would be useful to have a general understanding of the twin processes, frequently expounded in the writings of Shoghi Effendi, of disintegration and integration as they unfold in the world today.

I feel it would be helpful to look at the parable of the Lord of the vineyard, as given by Jesus Christ.

> A certain man planted a vineyard, and let it forth to husbandmen, and went into a far country for a long time. And at the season he sent a servant to the husbandmen, that they should give him of the fruit of the vineyard: but the husbandmen beat him, and sent him away empty. And again he sent another servant: and they beat him also, and entreated him shamefully, and sent him away empty. And again he sent a third: and they wounded him also, and cast him out. Then said the Lord of the vineyard, What shall I do? I will send my beloved son: it may be they will reverence him when they see him. But when the husbandmen saw him, they reasoned among themselves, saying, This is the heir: come, let us kill him, that the inheritance may be ours. So they cast him out of the vineyard, and killed him. What therefore shall the Lord of the vineyard do unto them? He shall come and destroy these husbandmen, and shall give the vineyard to others. (Luke 20:9–16)

Here are a few comments: (1) According to *God Passes By,* the Lord of the vineyard is a reference to Bahá'u'lláh. (2) The Son is obviously a reference to Jesus Christ, and the parable shows that Christ anticipated His own martyrdom. (3) The servants sent by the Lord are God's Prophets. We note that there is not only succession but progression in the degree of the authority they

1

wield. (4) The Father dismisses the tenants, who are obviously the religious and secular leaders, and He gives the vineyard to "others".

This final point leads us to our subject, namely, that the appearance of Bahá'u'lláh carries with it the dismantling of the old order and the establishment of a new system for the management of the vineyard. In other words, we see here the two processes of integration and disintegration. These twin processes are also envisaged in the New Testament, as we read in the Revelation of St John: "And I saw a new heaven and a new earth: for the first heaven and the first earth were passed away" (Revelation 21:1).

We find this theme embedded in the Writings of Bahá'u'lláh Himself. For example, He says on the one hand, "The time for the destruction of the world and its people hath arrived" (*Promised Day Is Come* ¶3), and, "From two ranks of men power hath been seized: kings and ecclesiastics" (¶37). At the same time He says, "The whole earth is now in a state of pregnancy. The day is approaching when it will have yielded its noblest fruits…" (¶8). He then joins the two processes together in one sentence, saying, "Soon will the present day Order be rolled up, and a new one spread out in its stead" (*World Order* 161).

We find 'Abdu'l-Bahá also referring to these two processes in His Writings: "The ills from which the world now suffers will multiply; the gloom which envelops it will deepen" (*World Order* 30). This is counterbalanced by, "Thus the world of humanity will be wholly transformed and the merciful bounties become manifest" (*Selections from the Writings of 'Abdu'l-Bahá* ¶224.1).

Shoghi Effendi gives us his description of the two processes in the following words:

> A two-fold process… can be distinguished, each tending, in its own way and with an accelerated momentum, to bring to a climax the forces that are transforming the face

of our planet. The first is essentially an integrating process, while the second is fundamentally disruptive. The former, as it steadily evolves, unfolds a System which may well serve as a pattern for that world polity towards which a strangely-disordered world is continually advancing; while the latter, as its disintegrating influence deepens, tends to tear down, with increasing violence, the antiquated barriers that seek to block humanity's progress towards its destined goal. The constructive process stands associated with the nascent Faith of Bahá'u'lláh, and is the harbinger of the New World Order that Faith must erelong establish. The destructive forces that characterize the other should be identified with a civilization that has refused to answer to the expectation of a new age, and is consequently falling into chaos and decline. (*World Order* 170)

It may be useful to form a mental image in our minds of these two processes which have their starting point in the year 1844. At the beginning, the two processes are seen to move along what appear to be parallel lines, one above the other. The higher line, which is the Faith, exerts its influence on the lower one, which in turn quite often reacts, consciously or unconsciously, in opposition. As this movement proceeds and the interaction intensifies, we see the two lines diverging from each other: the Faith in an upward flight and the world in a downward fall. In this connection the prophetic words of Shoghi Effendi are of utmost significance:

> The champion builders of Bahá'u'lláh's rising World Order must scale nobler heights of heroism as humanity plunges into greater depths of despair, degradation, dissension and distress. Let them forge ahead into the future serenely confident that the hour of their mightiest exertions and the supreme opportunity for their greatest exploits must coincide with the apocalyptic upheaval

marking the lowest ebb in mankind's fast-declining
fortunes. (*Citadel of Faith* 58)

The interaction has not stopped. We witness it under our very
eyes at this time in history.

The letters of Shoghi Effendi point to a new phenomenon.
They show that, almost imperceptibly, a third line between the
two that I have just described has been set in motion and is in
steady progress. This new line is a positive one and has come
into existence as an indirect impact of the Faith of God on the
minds and hearts of men. This new line represents the forces
which are in harmony with the spirit of the age, while its
protagonists are unconscious of the true source of this
constructive process.

This thought is clearly explained by Shoghi Effendi:

> The principle of the Oneness of Mankind... finds its
> earliest manifestations in the efforts consciously exerted
> and the modest beginnings already achieved by the
> declared adherents of the Faith of Bahá'u'lláh who... are
> forging ahead to establish His Kingdom on this earth. It
> has its indirect manifestations in the gradual diffusion of
> the spirit of world solidarity which is spontaneously arising
> out of the welter of a disorganized society. (*World Order*
> 43–4)

Shoghi Effendi also saw in the creation of the League of Nations
after the First World War a welcome by-product of this positive
development. He wrote,

> And yet while the shadows are continually deepening,
> might we not claim that gleams of hope, flashing
> intermittently on the international horizon, appear at times
> to relieve the darkness that encircles humanity? Would it
> be untrue to maintain that in a world of unsettled faith and

disturbed thought, a world of steadily mounting armaments, of unquenchable hatreds and rivalries, the progress, however fitful, of the forces working in harmony with the spirit of the age can already be discerned? Though the great outcry raised by post-war nationalism is growing louder and more insistent every day, the League of Nations is as yet in its embryonic state, and the storm clouds that are gathering may for a time totally eclipse its powers and obliterate its machinery, yet the direction in which the institution itself is operating is most significant... A general Pact on security has been the central purpose towards which these efforts have, ever since the League was born, tended to converge... For the first time in the history of humanity the system of collective security, foreshadowed by Bahá'u'lláh and explained by 'Abdu'l-Bahá, has been seriously envisaged, discussed and tested. (*World Order* 191–2)

Writing on the same theme, Shoghi Effendi describes the condition of the world as having been "contracted and transformed into a single highly complex organism by the marvellous progress achieved in the realm of physical science [and] by the world-wide expansion of commerce and industry" (*World Order* 47). He further points out that, by virtue of the "celestial potency which the Spirit of Bahá'u'lláh has breathed" into the world, "an increasing number of thoughtful men not only consider world peace as an approaching possibility, but as the necessary outcome of the forces now operating in the world" (47).

The League of Nations was replaced after the Second World War by the United Nations. Ever since its inception over half a century ago, it has been evolving positively in its spirit, fair judgement, and efficiency. There is no doubt that this middle process, brought into being with the inception of the Faith, will eventually lead to the Lesser Peace.

Shoghi Effendi has given us this definition of the Lesser Peace: "[This gradual process...] must, as Bahá'u'lláh has Himself anticipated, lead at first to the establishment of that Lesser Peace which the nations of the earth, as yet unconscious of His Revelation and yet unwittingly enforcing the general principles which He has enunciated, will themselves establish" (*Promised Day Is Come* ¶301). The Guardian further amplifies his own statement when he anticipates gradual steps in this process. These steps he identifies as "The political unification of the Eastern and Western Hemispheres,... the emergence of a world government and the establishment of the Lesser Peace as foreshadowed by the Prophet Isaiah" (*Citadel of Faith* 33). He further adds that this step involves "the reconstruction of mankind, as the result of the universal recognition of its oneness and wholeness..." (*Promised Day Is Come* ¶301).

The Words of Bahá'u'lláh on the subject of the Lesser Peace, as quoted by Shoghi Effendi in his writings, addressing the kings and rulers of the earth, are as follows:

> Now that ye have refused the Most Great Peace hold ye fast unto this the Lesser Peace, that haply ye may in some degree better your own condition and that of your dependants. Be reconciled among yourselves, that ye may need no more armaments save in a measure to safeguard your territories and dominions... (*World Order* 162).

> Be united, O concourse of the sovereigns of the world, for thereby will the tempest of discord be stilled amongst you, and your peoples find rest. Should any one among you take up arms against another, rise ye all against him, for this is naught but manifest justice (192).

In another Tablet He writes,

> The time must come when the imperative necessity for the holding of a vast, an all-embracing assemblage of men will

be universally realized. The rulers and kings of the earth must needs attend it, and, participating in its deliberations, must consider such ways and means as will lay the foundations of the world's Great Peace among men... Should any king take up arms against another, all should unitedly arise and prevent him. (*World Order* 192)

It is now important to focus our attention on the Most Great Peace and its features. Shoghi Effendi has given us the following definition:

The Most Great Peace... as conceived by Bahá'u'lláh—a peace that must inevitably follow as the practical consequence of the spiritualization of the world and the fusion of all its races, creeds, classes and nations—can rest on no other basis, and can be preserved through no other agency, except the divinely appointed ordinances that are implicit in the World Order that stands associated with His Holy Name. (*World Order* 162–3)

Shoghi Effendi further considers the following words, addressed to Queen Victoria by Bahá'u'lláh, to refer to the Most Great Peace and not to the Lesser Peace: "That which the Lord hath ordained as the sovereign remedy and mightiest instrument for the healing of the world is the union of all its peoples in one universal Cause, one common Faith. This can in no wise be achieved except through the power of a skilled, an all-powerful and inspired Physician. This, verily, is the truth, and all else naught but error..." (*World Order* 163). In another Tablet Bahá'u'lláh refers to the unity of all humankind. According to Shoghi Effendi, Bahá'u'lláh had in mind the Most Great Peace: "It beseemeth all men in this Day to take firm hold on the Most Great Name, and to establish the unity of all mankind. There is no place to flee to, no refuge that any one can seek, except Him" (163)

In the original texts, the term for the Lesser Peace is "Ṣulḥ-i-Aṣg͟har", and the term for the Most Great Peace "Ṣulḥ-i-Aʻẓam". In the original texts we find a third term used quite frequently, namely, "Ṣulḥ-i-Akbar". This is translated in various ways, at times as "the Lesser Peace", at others as "the Greater Peace", "the Great Peace", and even sometimes as "the Most Great Peace". It is most interesting that the beloved Guardian, in his capacity as interpreter of the Writings, has sometimes translated "Ṣulḥ-i-Akbar" as the "Lesser Peace" and at others as the "Most Great Peace", depending on the context. When one reads these carefully it becomes quite clear that whenever reference is made merely to the reduction of armaments, the need for consultation among nations, or the principle of collective security, Shoghi Effendi's translation is always the "Lesser Peace". However, when the context goes beyond political unification and deals with unity in all its aspects, including unity of race and of religion, the translation becomes the "Most Great Peace."

A careful reader will not find it difficult to conclude that "Ṣulḥ-i-Akbar" is a stage between the "Lesser" and the "Most Great Peace"—that is, between the "Aṣg͟har" and the "Aʻẓam". In my humble opinion the three stages can be encapsulated with the following terms used by him: "political unification" as the Lesser Peace, "spiritualization of the masses" as the intermediate stage, and the "fusion of races, creeds, classes and nations" as the Most Great Peace.

Suffice it to say at this point that it is clear to me that the superstate, with all its attendant institutions, described by Shoghi Effendi in "The Goal of the New World Order" (*World Order* 40–1), is a reference to this intermediate stage, namely, "Ṣulḥ-i-Akbar", while the features of the Bahá'í World Commonwealth, minutely and movingly described by Shoghi Effendi in "The Unfoldment of World Civilization" (203–4), are clear references to the "Ṣulḥ-i-Aʻẓam", that is, the Most Great Peace.

It is interesting to note in this connection that in his description of the world's superstate the first world body mentioned is the "International Executive", while in his illuminating description of the Most Great Peace the "World Executive" takes second place and the word "Legislature" first place. We could assume that the reason is that during the intermediary stage of "Ṣulḥ-i-Akbar" the spirit of the peace is certainly Bahá'í in its essence, but the outward form has to continue for a time to be the external structure of the old world.

In the world today the executive branch of government is usually, and even invariably, the leading entity and represents the headship of the state. In the Bahá'í concept of World Order, as I understand it, the hierarchy is different. Headship is vested not in the executive but in the legislative branch. That seems to be the reason why in Shoghi Effendi's description of the Bahá'í World Commonwealth of the future the first and primary entity is the "world legislature".

When we examine the Writings of 'Abdu'l-Bahá on this subject we find a similar pattern. A typical example is His Tablet of "The Seven Candles". This Tablet was revealed in 1906. This date is important because 'Abdu'l-Bahá refers in the Tablet to "this century" in connection to one of the candles, namely, the one on the "unity of nations", and it is clear that He was referring to the twentieth century.

The seven candles, as given by 'Abdu'l-Bahá, are (1) unity in the political realm, (2) unity of thought in world undertakings, (3) unity in freedom, (4) unity in religion, (5) unity of nations, (6) unity of races, and (7) unity of language. Five of the seven candles are, beyond any doubt, preliminary steps towards the Lesser Peace, whereas the fourth and sixth, namely, the unity of religions and of races, refer to forms of unity that can be achieved only when the spiritualization of the masses has taken place.

The first candle, for example, which is "unity in the political realm", has certainly been realized through the establishment of the United Nations. The third, being "unity in freedom", is surely a clear hint at the approaching end of colonization as it continued to exist during the first half of the century. The fifth, namely, "unity of nations", represents the spirit of world consciousness—expressed in the recognition that we are all, in the words of 'Abdu'l-Bahá about this candle, "citizens of one common fatherland"—a consciousness which was fully realized during the twentieth century. The significance of the remaining two candles, i.e. the second and the seventh, namely, "unity of thought in world undertakings" and "unity of language", are obvious and need no elaboration in this discussion.

As Bahá'ís, we have yet many challenges ahead of us to systematize our consolidation work through our institutes and study circles and to extend our teaching work through greater proclamation, more intense teaching activity, and closer adherence to living a Bahá'í way of life, collectively and individually. We should likewise open the doors of our homes and our community to seekers, sympathizers, and new friends of the Faith. Such activities are bound to generate waves of spiritual influence which will accelerate the constructive processes of integration pursued by well-meaning leaders of thought and men of goodwill everywhere as they move forward towards finding solutions to their economic, social, and political problems—problems that impede from time to time their advancement towards the goal set for them by the Blessed Beauty when, in His Tablets, He established the minimum requirements of the Lesser Peace.

To summarize what I have said and to project our thoughts into the future, perhaps we could suggest the following scenario: the world, its social fabric, its political configurations, its economic structure, and its moral standards will continue to deteriorate and will bring the current civilization to its lowest ebb. While on the one hand, we as Bahá'ís continue to expand the scope of our Faith, to consolidate its foundations, diffuse its light throughout the planet, and proclaim its life-giving message to the masses, and while on the other hand, the harmonizing forces which are activated and supported by the spirit of

Bahá'u'lláh's Message continue to develop, strike their roots into the soil of human consciousness, and eventually lead humanity to the universal prosperity generated by the Lesser Peace, we can well imagine that, later rather than sooner, the two integrative and parallel lines, namely, the Faith of God and its constructive worldly counterpart, will merge into one single, organically united, and divinely propelled process which will lead to the Most Great Peace and prepare the way for the establishment of the Kingdom of God on earth during the Golden Age of God's Holy Faith. In order to understand, perhaps with greater clarity, the different stages in the attainment of universal peace, so well defined by the progression implied in the adjectives qualifying the word "peace", namely, the Lesser, the Great or Greater, and the Most Great, corresponding to the words Aṣghar, Akbar, and A'ẓam in the original text, it may be useful for us to look at Shoghi Effendi's stages of the development of the Faith on the national level as it unfolds in different countries of the world.

Shoghi Effendi outlined seven stages for the onward march of the Faith in each country. I will mention the first four stages first. They are obscurity, repression, emancipation, and recognition. Stage one, which is obscurity, is clearly over throughout the world, as the House of Justice has also said. The Bahá'í community in Iran, as well as Bahá'í communities in a number of countries in the Middle East, is at stage two, which is repression. Stage three, namely, emancipation, is when the religious authorities in a country officially announce, as happened in Egypt, that since the Bahá'í Faith has laws and principles at variance with the canonical law of Islám it can only be considered as an independent entity, not as a branch of the Muḥammadan Faith. Stage four, namely, recognition, is when the government in authority recognizes the Faith in accordance with its own legal system; this is when the Bahá'í community is given status as a religious organization empowered to officially perform certain rites related to personal status, such as marriage. So far, this has been the highest form of recognition given in any country, as it represents the possession of a status equal to that enjoyed by other recognized religious communities. One or another of the first four stages could well be bypassed, and has indeed been bypassed, depending on the prevailing circumstances of a given country.

As to the last three stages, the fifth is the official acceptance of the Faith as the "State religion" of a nation (*Advent* 15). The sixth stage is when there is a merger between the civil system of government administration and the national institutions of the Bahá'í Administrative Order. This sixth stage has been described by Shoghi Effendi as the emergence of the "Bahá'í state" (15). The seventh stage is when the "Bahá'í state" of a given country joins hands with other Bahá'í states to form together the first Bahá'í Commonwealth—a Commonwealth which will represent the initial stages of the Most Great Peace and operate in accordance with the laws and principles enunciated by Bahá'u'lláh. As you can well realize, no Bahá'ís in any country have gone beyond stage four. This means that all national Bahá'í communities are developing slowly and sometimes painfully through the first four stages.

Moving from stage four to stage five will require, when circumstances permit, the input and guidance of the Universal House of Justice at their own appointed time. This is why Bahá'u'lláh has written, "All matters of State should be referred to the House of Justice..." (*Tablets of Bahá'u'lláh* 129). We can confidently conclude that, at the national level, stage five, namely, when the Faith is recognized as a "State religion", and stage six, namely, when the "Bahá'í State" emerges, correspond on the international level to the Great or Greater Peace, Ṣulḥ-i-Akbar, followed by the next stage, namely, the Most Great Peace, Ṣulḥ-i-A'ẓam. We firmly believe, as Bahá'ís, that the last two, and indeed the last three, stages are all part of the all-embracing, all-encompassing Major Plan of God.

Questions related:

Q. Shoghi Effendi has written that the years ahead may well be pregnant with events of unimaginable magnitude and ordeals more severe than what has transpired in the past. Are we "in the years ahead"? Should we be afraid?

A. The word "pregnant" implies a process. I have no doubt that we are in the so-called period of "the years ahead", but why should we be afraid? We should place our trust in Him, live the Bahá'í life, and face the future with full confidence. Faith is not enough; we should also have trust in Him. If we have doubts, we should arise and prove to ourselves the reality of His assistance. In one of his letters to the American believers Shoghi Effendi said, "There is no time to lose... The stage is set. The firm and irrevocable Promise is given. God's own Plan has been set in motion... The powers of heaven and earth mysteriously assist in its execution... Let the doubter arise, and himself verify the truth of such assertions." (*This Decisive Hour* ¶46.5)

Q. What is "the Most Great Justice"?

A. I think this is a reference to the institutions of the House of Justice on its three levels: universal, national, and local.

Q. Is entry by troops important to the Lesser Peace?

A. I do not see it that way. Entry by troops is an internal process in the development of the teaching work. The House of Justice wishes us to prepare ourselves through the institutes, study circles, devotional meetings, and children's classes to open our doors for the troops to come in and be adequately and systematically deepened in the Cause. Shoghi Effendi's writings indicate that this stage of entry by troops will prove to be a prelude to the conversion of the masses.

The Lesser Peace, however, is the result of the efforts of leaders in the political world uniting at last to establish what we could call a secular political peace among the nations.

Q. Do we know when the Lesser Peace will come about? Why did we think it would be by the year 2000?

A. When Shoghi Effendi was asked when exactly the Lesser Peace would be established, he wrote back saying that we did not know the exact time. The speculation about the year 2000 stems from the fifth candle of unity, which is "unity of nations", and, as you recall, 'Abdu'l-Bahá states in that Tablet that it is "a unity which in this century will be securely established" (*World Order* 39). Since this Tablet was revealed in 1906, it is obvious that "this century" means the twentieth century, especially since the recipient was one of the friends in the British Isles. The point that was missed was that the stage of the "unity of nations" is clearly defined by 'Abdu'l-Bahá Himself in the same Tablet. It is when "the peoples of the world [will] regard themselves as citizens of one common fatherland" (39). This is a reference to an awareness in the peoples of the world that the world is really one world and the planet the home of the human race. This consciousness is, of course, an important step towards the Lesser Peace but not the Lesser Peace itself.

Q. What is the relationship between the seven stages in the evolution of the Faith and the seven candles of unity?

A. These are two processes. One is related to the internal development of the Faith within the setting of the world surrounding it, and the other is a description of the various aspects of the universal peace anticipated in the Writings.

Q. When the Faith becomes the official established religion of a country, will independent investigation of truth continue to be upheld?

A. The principle of independent investigation of truth is an overarching principle which overshadows the entire Dispensation. The Báb tells us that God's method for the spread of His religion at any given time was never meant to be through force or coercion (*Selections from the Writings of the Báb* 77).

Q. What is the meaning of Shoghi Effendi's statement, in his "Unfoldment", that "the Revelation of Bahá'u'lláh should be viewed as marking the last and highest stage in this stupendous evolution of man's collective life on this planet"?

A. Shoghi Effendi has likened the process of world federalism to the stages that led the American Republic to become a unified community of federated states. He describes the latter process as an event which proclaimed the coming of age of the American people. He goes on to state:

> Within the territorial limits of this nation, this consummation may be viewed as the culmination of the process of human government. The diversified and loosely related elements of a divided community were brought together, unified and incorporated in one coherent system. Though this entity may continue gaining in cohesive power, though the unity already achieved may be further consolidated, though the civilization to which that unity could alone have given birth may expand and flourish, yet the machinery essential to such an unfoldment may be said to have been, in its essential structure, erected, and the impulse required to guide and sustain it may be regarded as having been fundamentally imparted. No stage above and

15

beyond this consummation of national unity can, within the geographical limits of that nation, be imagined, though the highest destiny of its people, as a constituent element in a still larger entity that will embrace the whole of mankind, may still remain unfulfilled. Considered as an isolated unit, however, this process of integration may be said to have reached its highest and final consummation. (*World Order* 165)

As with the geographical limits of one nation, so it will be within the geographical limits of the planet. It is in this vein that the following words of Shoghi Effendi, referring to the emergence of a world community, should be understood:

The Revelation of Bahá'u'lláh... should be viewed... as marking the last and highest stage in this stupendous evolution of man's collective life on this planet. The emergence of a world community, the consciousness of world citizenship, the founding of a world civilization and culture... should, by their very nature, be regarded, as far as this planetary life is concerned, as the furthermost limits in the organization of human society, though man, as an individual, will, nay must indeed as a result of such a consummation, continue indefinitely to progress and develop. (*World Order* 163)

Q. Bahá'u'lláh says, "Should any one among you take up arms against another, rise ye [i.e. sovereigns of the world] against him for this is naught but manifest justice" (*World Order* 40). Is there such an option under the Most Great Peace?

A. If we read the antecedent to this sentence in the original, it becomes clear that this guidance regarding the principle of collective security is written in the context of the Lesser Peace. It appears highly unlikely that such a situation would arise under the Most Great Peace. If it did, however, the instruction of Bahá'u'lláh would certainly be immediately enforced.

Q. Where does the line of disintegration lead to, and will it finally disappear?

A. I spoke about the two opposite and diverging lines of integration and disintegration, the former symbolizing the growth and consolidation of the Faith and the latter representing the deterioration and decline of human society. What we should remember is that, according to Bahá'u'lláh, we are approaching the stage of humanity's maturity. This maturity has been described by Shoghi Effendi in these words:

> That mystic, all pervasive, yet indefinable change, which we associate with the stage of maturity inevitable in the life of the individual and the development of the fruit must... have its counterpart in the evolution of the organization of human society... Such a stage of maturity in the process of human government must, for all time, if we would faithfully recognize the tremendous claim advanced by Bahá'u'lláh, remain identified with the Revelation of which He was the Bearer. (*World Order* 163–4)

> To take but one instance. How confident were the assertions made in the days preceding the unification of the states of the North American continent regarding the insuperable barriers that stood in the way of their ultimate federation! ...Could anything less than the fire of a civil war with all its violence and vicissitudes—a war that nearly rent the great American Republic—have welded the states, not only into a Union of independent units, but into a Nation, in spite of all the ethnic differences that

. characterized its component parts?... That nothing short of the fire of a severe ordeal, unparalleled in its intensity, can fuse and weld the discordant entities that constitute the elements of present-day civilization, into the integral components of the world commonwealth of the future, is a truth which future events will increasingly demonstrate. (*World Order* 45–6)

As we see in the quotations above, universal suffering is a prerequisite for universal spiritual awareness. To the observations quoted above from the pen of Shoghi Effendi I feel I should add the following momentous pronouncement by him.

The process of disintegration must inexorably continue, and its corrosive influence must penetrate deeper and deeper into the very core of a crumbling age. Much suffering will still be required ere the contending nations, creeds, classes and races of mankind are fused in the crucible of universal affliction... Adversities unimaginably appalling, undreamed of crises and upheavals, war, famine and pestilence, might well combine to engrave in the soul of an unheeding generation those truths and principles which it has disdained to recognize and follow. (*World Order* 193)

According to a Tablet revealed by 'Abdu'l-Bahá, the line of disintegration propelling the world towards godlessness will sink to such a point that it will lead to universal chaos and confusion—a chaotic condition that the world would be unwilling to bear. This stage will lead the world to turn to religion and realize the importance of turning to God. That will be the time when the Bahá'í youth of today will have the unique opportunity to proclaim and teach the Cause of Bahá'u'lláh, as a far greater receptivity to His message would prevail in the hearts of men everywhere. It is quite possible, in my view, that at such a time, the stage of mass conversion anticipated in the writings of Shoghi Effendi would occur and would result in a sudden "thousandfold" increase in the "numerical strength as well as the material power and the spiritual authority of the Faith of Bahá'u'lláh" (*Citadel of Faith* 117).

Q. When does the Bahá'í community move from the stage of "recognition" to the stage of "State Religion" in any given country?

A. Shoghi Effendi refers to the "majority" of a country's population (*World Order* 7). He does not define how large a majority this should be. As it is a matter of "State" when such a situation arises, it should be referred to the Universal House of Justice.

Q. When a "Bahá'í State" is established in a particular country, will non-Bahá'ís have the right to vote and/or occupy positions in the administration of the State?

A. All I can say is that this issue has not been dealt with in the Writings of our Faith and, therefore, should be referred to the Universal House of Justice in accordance with His statement, already mentioned above, "All matters of State should be referred to the House of Justice" (*Tablets of Bahá'u'lláh* 27).

Q. In addition to the United Nations, which you have mentioned, what do you think of such organizations as the European Union, the World Bank, and the International Monetary Fund?

A. All these are manifestations of humanity's awareness of its own universal solidarity, and, as 'Abdu'l-Bahá has predicted in His second "candle of unity", humanity is moving steadily towards "unity of thought in world undertakings" (*World Order*

19

39). The examples you cite are few among many examples of efforts to create projects that promote the welfare of all classes, races, and nations that comprise the world community. Other examples are WHO, UNESCO, UNICEF, the Red Cross, and the various agencies which are operating today to protect the environment, research the oceans, explore the solar system, promote the positive values of globalization, eradicate illiteracy, etc. Such world undertakings did not exist in the past, but these ideals have been earnestly and successfully pursued for the first time, on a global scale, from the early beginnings of the twentieth century. This is why 'Abdu'l-Bahá called it the "Century of Light". Furthermore, we see Bahá'u'lláh exhorting and, indeed, giving a special mission to the rulers of the entire western hemisphere, addressing them as leaders of one geographical unit. Does this not imply a process of solidarity of the components parts of this unit? Many efforts have already been made towards this objective, although they have met with setbacks and reverses. Shoghi Effendi, following Bahá'u'lláh's lead, likewise refers to the eastern hemisphere as a counterpart to the western hemisphere (*Citadel of Faith* 33) and specifically mentions the prospect of the political unification of the two hemispheres as a stage towards the establishment of world peace. Shoghi Effendi has described for us the stages of humanity's social evolution towards its maturity in the following inspired words:

> The long ages of infancy and childhood, through which the human race had to pass, have receded into the background. Humanity is now experiencing the commotions invariably associated with the most turbulent stage of its evolution, the stage of adolescence, when the impetuosity of youth and its vehemence reach their climax, and must gradually be superseded by the calmness, the wisdom, and the maturity that characterize the stage of manhood. Then will the human race reach that stature of ripeness which will enable it to acquire all the powers and

capacities upon which its ultimate development must depend. Unification of the whole of mankind is the hallmark of the stage which human society is now approaching. Unity of family, of tribe, of city-state, and nation have been successively attempted and fully established. World unity is the goal towards which a harassed humanity is striving. Nation-building has come to an end. The anarchy inherent in state sovereignty is moving towards a climax. A world, growing to maturity, must abandon this fetish, recognize the oneness and wholeness of human relationships, and establish once for all the machinery that can best incarnate this fundamental principle of its life. (*World Order* 202)

THE GUARDIANSHIP AND THE UNIVERSAL HOUSE OF JUSTICE
UNDER THE PROVISIONS OF THE KITÁB-I-AQDAS
AND 'ABDU'L-BAHÁ'S WILL AND TESTAMENT

Shoghi Effendi has singled out Bahá'u'lláh's Kitáb-i-Aqdas and 'Abdu'l-Bahá's Will and Testament as chief depositories "wherein are enshrined those priceless elements of that Divine Civilization, the establishment of which is the primary mission of the Bahá'í Faith" (*World Order* 3–4) and as the "twin repositories of the constituent elements" of the "Sovereignty which the Bahá'í teachings foreshadow" (16). He furthermore describes the Kitáb-i-Aqdas as the "Charter of the future world civilization" (*God Passes By* 214). He calls the Will and Testament of 'Abdu'l-Bahá by exactly the same title (328).

We should be aware that when the Friends in Iran read the Kitáb-i-Aqdas for the first time, they regarded it, albeit with great reverence, merely as Bahá'u'lláh's Mother Book or the Book of His Laws, just as the Qur'án was the Mother Book for the Muslim world. Some of the verses of the Aqdas were not understood and were even, alas, misunderstood. For example, the celebrated passage in the Kitáb-i-Aqdas announcing the emergence of the new World Order was understood to mean that the order of the verses of the Aqdas followed a unique pattern different from that of the Bayán or Sacred Books of former Dispensations.

There is also in the Persian Bayán a verse which refers to the Order of Bahá'u'lláh. This corresponding verse in the Bayán foreshadowing the Order of Bahá'u'lláh was also understood along the same lines, namely, that Bahá'u'lláh's Mother Book, unlike the Bayán, would not be divided into chapters and verses but would have a unique format of its own. It was only in 1934, some 13 years after the launching of the institution of the Guardianship, that Shoghi Effendi produced his translation of this key verse in Bahá'u'lláh's Mother Book. For the first time it became clear to the Bahá'ís in the East and the West that the Order mentioned had nothing to do with the style or format of the Kitáb-i-Aqdas but was instead an announcement that the Revelation of Bahá'u'lláh was the begetter of a new world system for the conduct of the affairs of the world and the establishment of the promised Kingdom of God on earth.

As to the Will and Testament of 'Abdu'l-Bahá, the Bahá'ís in both the East and the West considered it a document in which the Covenant of Bahá'u'lláh was being extended by 'Abdu'l-Bahá to cover the line of succession after His passing. In Shoghi Effendi the Bahá'ís of the world saw the successor of 'Abdu'l-Bahá. He would henceforth be the Interpreter of the Divine Word and the Centre of the Cause to whom all must turn. All this was of course true, but it was only a simplistic and minimal appraisal of what Shoghi Effendi later described as the "Charter of the future world civilization".

Shoghi Effendi lifted the veil gradually. For example, in 1923, barely two years after the passing of 'Abdu'l-Bahá, he described the contents of His Will and Testament as "amazing in all its aspects" and its provisions as having "challenged and perplexed the keenest minds" (*Bahá'í Administration* 50). Writing in the same year to the friends in Persia, he wrote,

God's Supreme House of Justice shall be erected and firmly established in the days to come. When this most great Edifice shall be reared... God's purpose, wisdom, universal truths, mysteries and realities of the Kingdom, which the mystic revelation of Bahá'u'lláh has deposited within the Will and Testament of 'Abdu'l-Bahá, shall gradually be revealed and made manifest. (*Messages from the Universal House of Justice* ¶23.22c)

A year later he wrote,

> We are called upon by our beloved Master in His Will and Testament not only to adopt it [Bahá'u'lláh's new World Order] unreservedly, but to unveil its merit to all the world. To attempt to estimate its full value, and grasp its exact significance after so short a time since its inception would be premature and presumptuous on our part. We must trust to time, and the guidance of God's Universal House of Justice, to obtain a clearer and fuller understanding of its ['Abdu'l-Bahá's Will and Testament's] provisions and implications. (*Bahá'í Administration* 62)

And some five years later, in 1929, he called it the chief depository enshrining the priceless elements of God's Divine Civilization and added the following comment:

> We stand indeed too close to so monumental a document to claim for ourselves a complete understanding of all its implications, or to presume to have grasped the manifold mysteries it undoubtedly contains. Only future generations can comprehend the value and the significance attached to this Divine Masterpiece, which the hand of the Master-builder of the world has designed for the unification and the triumph of the world-wide Faith of Bahá'u'lláh. (*World Order* 8)

Shoghi Effendi did not stop there; he continued in his assessment and praise of the manifold mysteries contained in 'Abdu'l-Bahá's Will and Testament. About a year later, on 25 March 1930, his comments about the hidden mysteries of the Will and Testament of 'Abdu'l-Bahá reached their crescendo when, in a letter written on his behalf, he pointed out the following: "The contents of the Will of the Master are far too much for the present generation to comprehend. It needs at least a century of actual working before the treasures of wisdom hidden in it can be revealed..." (*Messages from the Universal House of Justice* ¶75.18).

The friends were wondering where the mysteries could be. Could these relate to their own limited understanding of the station of the Guardianship? Were the mysteries in relation to the functions of the Universal House of Justice? Why should it take so long for Bahá'ís to understand what appeared to them to be a straightforward document about the future administration of the Faith? I will now deal with these questions.

Shoghi Effendi says that the provisions of the two charters, namely, the Kitáb-i-Aqdas and the Will and Testament of 'Abdu'l-Bahá, are neither incompatible nor contradictory and indeed "mutually confirm one another, and are inseparable parts of one complete unit" (*World Order* 4). However, a basic outward contradiction between the two documents did exist, because the Kitáb-i-Aqdas envisages a time when there will be no Aghṣáns, meaning thereby that there would be no future Guardians, while the Will and Testament of 'Abdu'l-Bahá provided for a succession of Guardians.

The verse in the Kitáb-i-Aqdas that refers to the Aghṣáns reads as follows:

Endowments dedicated to charity revert to God... None hath the right to dispose of them without leave from Him Who is the Dawning-place of Revelation. After Him, this authority shall pass to the Aghṣáns, and after them to the House of Justice—should it be established in the world by then... Otherwise, the endowments shall revert to the people of Bahá who speak not except by His leave and judge not save in accordance with what God hath decreed in this Tablet... (¶42)

In explanation of this verse, notes 66 and 67 of the Kitáb-i-Aqdas read as follows:

"Aghsán" (plural of Ghusn) is the Arabic word for "Branches". This term is used by Bahá'u'lláh to designate His male descendants. It has particular implications not only for the disposition of endowments but also for the succession of authority following the passing of Bahá'u'lláh... and of 'Abdu'l-Bahá. Bahá'u'lláh, in the Book of His Covenant, appointed 'Abdu'l-Bahá, His eldest son, as the Centre of His Covenant and the Head of the Faith. Abdu'l-Bahá, in His Will and Testament, appointed Shoghi Effendi, His eldest grandson, as the Guardian and Head of the Faith. This passage of the Aqdas, therefore, anticipates the succession of chosen Aghsán and thus the institution of the Guardianship and envisages the possibility of a break in their line. The passing of Shoghi Effendi in 1957 precipitated the very situation provided for in this passage, in that the line of Aghsán ended before the Universal House of Justice had been established... (Note 66)

Bahá'u'lláh provides for the possibility that the line of Aghsán would terminate prior to the establishment of the Universal House of Justice. He designated that in such a situation "endowments shall revert to the people of Bahá". The term "people of Bahá" is used with a number of different meanings in the Bahá'í Writings. In this instance, they are described as those "who speak not except by His leave and judge not save in accordance with what God hath decreed in this Tablet". Following the passing of Shoghi Effendi in 1957, the Hands of the Cause of God directed the affairs of the Cause until the election of the Universal House of Justice in 1963... (Note 67)

An important point about the Aghsáns needs some clarification. In the Writings of Bahá'u'lláh and 'Abdu'l-Bahá, there is a clear distinction made between Aghsáns who are appointed as Heads of the Faith and Interpreters of its teachings and the rest of the Aghṣáns who do not fall into this category. Regarding the latter group of Aghṣáns, we read the following from the Pen of Bahá'u'lláh in His Kitáb-i-'Ahd: "It is enjoined upon everyone to manifest love towards the Aghṣáns, but God hath not granted them any right to the property of others" (*Tablets of Bahá'u'lláh* 222). The prohibition to claim certain rights relates to the practice allowed in some sects of Islám of granting prerogatives to the descendants of the Prophet Muḥammad to claim financial privileges for themselves.

The Will and Testament clearly states, "It is incumbent upon the guardian of the Cause of God to appoint within his own life-time him that may be his successor that differences shall not arise after his passing" (*Bahá'í Administration* 8). Furthermore, the Will states that the Guardian of the Cause of God is the Universal House of Justice's "sacred head" and the "distinguished member for life" of that body. The Will further stipulates,

> The Hands of The Cause of God must elect from their own number nine persons that shall at all times be occupied in the important services in the work of the guardian of the Cause of God... [These], whether unanimously or by a majority vote, must give their assent to the choice of the one whom the guardian of the Cause of God hath chosen as his successor. (*Bahá'í Administration* 10)

An amazing feature of the Will is its flexibility. On the one hand it provides for a Universal House of Justice with a Guardian heading its membership, and on the other, in the same document, the Author of the Will envisages a Universal House of Justice that is equally divinely guided but without the physical presence or membership of a Guardian. From two passages in the Will and Testament of 'Abdu'l-Bahá, it becomes clear that the elected members of the Universal House of Justice receive

27

independent divine guidance—guidance which is not conditioned upon the presence of the Guardian as sacred Head of that institution. The first reference is as follows:

> [The] Guardian of the Cause of God, as well as the Universal House of Justice to be universally elected and established, are both under the care and protection of the Abhá Beauty, under the shelter and unerring guidance of His Holiness the Exalted One... Whatsoever they decide is of God. Whoso obeyeth him not, neither obeyeth them, has not obeyed God... (*Will and Testament* 11)

The second reference is incorporated in the second part of 'Abdu'l-Bahá's Will, written most probably in 1907. Here are His own words: "I am now in very great danger and the hope of even an hour's life is lost to me. I am thus constrained to write these lines for the protection of the Cause of God, the preservation of His Law, the safeguarding of His Word and the safety of His Teachings" (*Will and Testament* 19).

In this portion of the Will, written when Shoghi Effendi was only about 10 years old and during a period which Shoghi Effendi later described as "the darkest moments of [the Master's] life, under 'Abdu'l-Ḥamíd's regime, when He stood ready to be deported to the most inhospitable regions of Northern Africa" (*World Order* 17) , 'Abdu'l-Bahá wrote the following:

> Unto the Most Holy Book every one must turn, and all that is not expressly recorded therein must be referred to the Universal House of Justice. That which this body, whether unanimously or by a majority doth carry, that is verily the truth and the purpose of God Himself. Whoso doth deviate therefrom is verily of them that love discord, hath shown forth malice, and turned away from the Lord of the Covenant. By this House is meant that Universal House of Justice which is to be elected from all countries, that is

from those parts in the East and West where the loved ones are to be found... It is incumbent upon these members (of the Universal House of Justice) to gather in a certain place and deliberate upon all problems which have caused difference, questions that are obscure and matters that are not expressly recorded in the Book. Whatsoever they decide has the same effect as the Text itself. (*Will and Testament* 19)

As indicated by the Universal House of Justice in its letter of 9 March 1965 (*Messages from the Universal House of Justice* ¶23.15), it was also at this very time that 'Abdu'l-Bahá wrote to the cousin of the Báb, the chief builder of the 'Ishqábád Temple, Hájí Mírzá Taqí Afnán, a Tablet in which He describes the dangers to His life and adds that He has written a Will and Testament in which He has given directions for the election of the Universal House of Justice. He instructs him in that Tablet to come therefore to the Holy Land should the threats against Him materialize, open His Will and Testament, and carry out His wishes.

These precautionary measures taken by 'Abdu'l-Bahá, however, were never realized. The coup of the Young Turks overthrew the Ottoman monarchy, 'Abdu'l-Bahá was released from prison, and intense activity on His part followed for over a decade. Could we not assume, therefore, that in accordance with God's inscrutable Purpose all this happened so that 'Abdu'l-Bahá could, in a natural and matter-of-fact way, leave for posterity His clear testimony that the Universal House of Justice could certainly operate fully without the physical presence of the Guardian as its Head?

The fact that the Universal House of Justice, with only its elected members, will be the direct and independent recipient of Divine guidance throughout this Dispensation is further confirmed by the words of Shoghi Effendi in "The Dispensation of Bahá'u'lláh":

In the conduct of the administrative affairs of the Faith, in the enactment of the legislation necessary to supplement the laws of the Kitáb-i-Aqdas, the members of the Universal House of Justice... are to follow in a prayerful attitude, the dictates and promptings of their conscience... They, and not the body who either directly or indirectly elect them, have thus been made the recipients of the divine guidance which is at once the life-blood and ultimate safeguard of this Revelation. (*World Order* 153)

In the light of what occurred after the passing of Shoghi Effendi, who neither left a will nor appointed in his own lifetime a Branch to be his successor (an appointment that was to have been confirmed by nine elected Hands residing in the Holy Land), it became clear to the Hands of the Cause of God and the entire Bahá'í world that the second possibility provided by the provisions of the Will was indeed inevitable and fully compatible not only with the Will itself but also with the provisions of the Kitáb-i-Aqdas.

It would be useful at this point for us to review briefly the contents of the Will and Testament of 'Abdu'l-Bahá in the light of the provisions of Bahá'u'lláh's "Book of the Covenant". The Book of the Covenant is published in full in "Tablets of Bahá'u'lláh revealed after the Kitáb-i-Aqdas", pages 217 to 223. In this document, known as the Kitáb-i-'Ahd, Bahá'u'lláh clearly appoints 'Abdu'l-Bahá, the Most Great Branch, as His successor. But then He goes on to say, "Verily God hath ordained the station of the Greater Branch [Muḥammad-'Alí] to be beneath that of the Most Great Branch ['Abdu'l-Bahá]...We have chosen 'the Greater' after 'the Most Great'..." (*Tablets of Bahá'u'lláh* 222). This means that, after 'Abdu'l-Bahá, Muḥammad-'Alí, half-brother of 'Abdu'l-Bahá, would be the Centre of the Cause, provided of course that he would be firm in the Covenant and realize that his station was beneath the exalted position reserved

THE GUARDIANSHIP AND THE UNIVERSAL HOUSE OF JUSTICE

for the Master. However, even before the interment of the sacred remains of Bahá'u'lláh, when 'Abdu'l-Bahá was washing His Father's body with His own hands, Muḥammad-'Alí, his brothers, and his brother-in-law, as well as members of their immediate family, leagued together to oppose 'Abdu'l-Bahá. Their first act of disloyalty was to steal the two cases which contained documents and papers entrusted by Bahá'u'lláh to the care of 'Abdu'l-Bahá, including a number of His seals. Muḥammad-'Alí subsequently embarked on a series of attacks on the person of 'Abdu'l-Bahá by sending letters, followed by emissaries, to establish his right as the one mentioned in Bahá'u'lláh's Will and to discredit 'Abdu'l-Bahá, Who, as alleged by him, had claimed the station of the Manifestation of God. We should recall that Muḥammad-'Alí had, during the Ministry of his Father, already advanced the claim of being God's "finger", "the spokesman of the Aghṣán", and "the upholder of the Holy Writ" (*God Passes By* 248–49). For making such claims as these, Bahá'u'lláh personally slapped Muḥammad-'Alí in the face with His own hand (249).

In one of His Tablets to the friends in Iran, Bahá'u'lláh explicitly rules out the assignment of any spiritual station to Muḥammad-'Alí and adds the categorical statement, "Should he for a moment pass out from under the shadow of the Cause, he surely shall be brought to naught" (*Will and Testament* 6). 'Abdu'l-Bahá, in His Will and Testament, quotes this passage from Bahá'u'lláh's Tablet, enumerates the acts of disloyalty by His half-brother, including his plot to assassinate Him, and irrefutably draws the conclusion that Muḥammad-'Alí had broken the Covenant and had thus disqualified himself from being second in succession to Him.

Many of these violations came to be known during 'Abdu'l-Bahá's lifetime to the friends in Iran. A few had asked what would happen after His passing. Sometimes He would say that the Universal House of Justice would be formed. At other times

He would state that this was a "secret" and that "the time will come when its light will appear" (*World Order* 150).

Amatu'l-Bahá Rúḥíyyih Khánum, in *The Priceless Pearl*, quotes the recollections of a German woman physician, Dr J. Fallscheer, who lived in Haifa and attended to the ladies of 'Abdu'l-Bahá's household. In these recollections, which were first published in German, she says that the Greatest Holy Leaf had informed her that Shoghi Effendi was destined to be the successor of the Master. One day, in August 1910, after the young Shoghi Effendi left the room of the Master, 'Abdu'l-Bahá turned to Dr Fallscheer and told her,

> How do you like my future Elisha?... And do you know why? ...Bahá'u'lláh... the blessed Manifestation reminded me that I... must observe among my sons and grandsons whom God would indicate... My sons passed to eternity in their tenderest years, in my line, among my relatives, only little Shoghi has the shadow of a great calling in the depths of his eyes. (*Priceless Pearl* 11–12)

I cannot refrain from sharing with you at this juncture the fact that there was a private belief current among some of the early believers in Iran that, since Muḥammad-'Alí had broken the Covenant, 'Abdu'l-Bahá would had to have chosen one of His grandsons to be His successor. This was not because of Dr Fallscheer's reminiscences, which were obviously not available in Persian; they had arrived at this assumption on the basis of the contents of the Tablet of the Holy Mariner. In this Tablet, three figures prominently emerge: (1) The Holy Mariner, namely, Bahá'u'lláh Himself; (2) The Maid of Heaven, who flooded "with the light of her countenance the heaven and the earth" (*Bahá'í Prayers* 54), namely, 'Abdu'l-Bahá; and (3) One of the handmaidens of the Maid of Heaven, who is also described as the "favoured damsel" who "perfumed all things in the lands of holiness and grandeur" (*Bahá'í Prayers* 55), namely, Shoghi

Effendi. These speculations acquired added importance when, in one of His last Tablets, 'Abdu'l-Bahá wrote, "Study the Tablet of the Holy Mariner that ye may know the truth, and consider that the Blessed Beauty hath fully foretold future events. Let them who perceive, take warning!" (*Bahá'í Prayers* 51).

We should now turn our attention to the Law of Succession as it was applied not only to Shoghi Effendi as Guardian of the Faith but also to the Administrative Order, which Shoghi Effendi quite often referred to as "The Child of the Covenant" (*God Passes By* 243). It should be recalled, however, that in one instance Shoghi Effendi also described the Will and Testament of 'Abdu'l-Bahá as the "Child of the Covenant"—a Child which was born from the interaction of the creative energies of the Law of Bahá'u'lláh on the mind of 'Abdu'l-Bahá. We should not be perturbed by the fact that the term "Child of the Covenant" has been used to describe the charter of the Administrative Order as well as the Order itself. The one is the establishment of the entity in the Holy Writ, and the other is the emergence of that reality for all to see.

In this connection, we should remember that the Bahá'í Covenant is not something which began and ended with the Ministry of 'Abdu'l-Bahá. While 'Abdu'l-Bahá was the Centre of the Covenant and will continue to be so for all time, the Bahá'í Covenant is an essential feature inseparable from the Faith of Bahá'u'lláh until the end of this Dispensation. In fact, in one of His Tablets, 'Abdu'l-Bahá refers to His Ministry as "The Morn" of the Bahá'í Covenant. This implies that the unfoldment of the Covenant in its fullness, throughout the Day of Bahá'u'lláh's Dispensation, was yet to come. This important point is explained by Shoghi Effendi:

As regards the meaning of the Bahá'í Covenant: The Guardian considers the existence of two forms of covenant both of which are explicitly mentioned in the literature of the Cause. First is the covenant that every Prophet makes with humanity or, more definitely, with His people that they will accept and follow the coming Manifestation Who will be the reappearance of His reality. The second form of covenant is such as the one Bahá'u'lláh made with His people that they should accept the Master. This is merely to establish and strengthen the succession of the series of Lights that appear after every Manifestation. Under the same category falls the covenant the Master made with the Bahá'ís that they should accept His administration after Him... (*Lights of Guidance* no. 593)

From the above text it is clear that the successor to the Master under the Bahá'í Covenant is the administration after Him. It is in this light that we should understand the term used by Shoghi Effendi describing the Guardianship and the Universal House of Justice as the "chosen Successors" of Bahá'u'lláh and 'Abdu'l-Bahá (*World Order* 20). We should recall that the term "Administrative Order" was used by Shoghi Effendi for the first time in his "Dispensation", which was written in February 1934. During the first 13 years of his Guardianship, that is, from 1921 to 1934, he referred to the System conceived by Bahá'u'lláh for the administration of His Cause as the "Bahá'í Administration". As the letter that I have just quoted from Shoghi Effendi about the Bahá'í Covenant is dated 1932, we should clearly understand therefore that what he meant by the "administration after Him" was the Administrative Order.

In "The Dispensation of Bahá'u'lláh", Shoghi Effendi points out that the Administrative Order has two pillars: the Guardianship and the Universal House of Justice. One way of understanding the word "pillars" is that there are two columns, and a structure is placed on them. Thus, if one of them is removed, the structure will be lopsided and fall. But when one reads with diligence and care the writings of Shoghi Effendi, we see that what he meant by "pillars" were institutions which reinforced the stability of the structure.

For example, in "The Dispensation", he refers to these twin institutions as means provided to "buttress" the structure of the Administrative Order (*World Order* 157). To "buttress" means to provide support and strength to a structure. There are other metaphors that Shoghi Effendi uses for these institutions. For example, in one of his messages, he describes the Guardianship as "the head cornerstone of the Administrative Order" (*This Decisive Hour* ¶27.1). The relation of the cornerstone to a structure is different from that of a pillar or a buttress to the structure. The cornerstone of a building is a foundation and indispensable stone—the first block—used as a basis for the erection of the structure.

As regards the Universal House of Justice, the metaphors of "pillar" and "buttress" equally apply to that institution; but, using the same concept of a building, he describes the Universal House of Justice as "the apex of the Bahá'í Administrative Order" (*God Passes By* 332). He also refers to it as the "crowning glory" of the administrative institutions of the Faith (*Advent* 29), "the supreme organ of the Bahá'í Commonwealth" (*World Order* 7), as well as "the last refuge of a tottering civilization" (89). Although not all of us are architects, we can all easily understand that the first unit in the building of a structure is its cornerstone, and its last unit is the apex. It is interesting in this connection to recall that in one of his Persian letters to the friends in the East he refers to the Guardianship as the "first pillar" and the Universal House of Justice as the "second". This could mean the first in rank or the first in time. In terms of the timeline, this is exactly what happened. When one Successor, namely, the Guardian, was providentially removed from the scene, the other Successor, namely, the Universal House of Justice, was naturally and inevitably expected to assume the Headship of the Cause.

When we discuss the two institutions of the Guardianship and the Universal House of Justice, we tend to be perplexed by two paragraphs in "The Dispensation" which underline the essential features of these two Successors to the Founders of our

Faith. One paragraph begins, "Divorced from the institution of the Guardianship the World Order of Bahá'u'lláh would be mutilated"; the other paragraph begins, "Severed from the no less essential institution of the Universal House of Justice this same System... would be paralyzed" (*World Order* 148). These two paragraphs, in the light of the reality of what happened after the passing of Shoghi Effendi, who neither wrote a Will nor appointed someone after him to occupy the seat of the Guardianship, would obviously mean that the World Order of Bahá'u'lláh without any Guardian would have resulted in the mutilation of the World Order, just as that same World Order would have been paralyzed if it did not have any Universal House of Justice to supplement the Laws of Bahá'u'lláh. But since we have had 36 years of the institution of the Guardianship operating in full and intensive action, and we now have the Universal House of Justice, the structure of the World Order is neither mutilated nor paralyzed.

There could well be a lingering thought remaining in some minds as to why Shoghi Effendi left no will. Was it an accident or a conscious action on his part? From Violette Nakhjavání's *Tribute to Amatu'l-Bahá Rúḥíyyih Khánum*, we gather that Shoghi Effendi, towards the end of his life and contemplating his own death, gave advice to Amatu'l-Bahá regarding the travels she should undertake after his own passing. He is also reported to have told her during the last remaining days of his life in London that he did not want to go back to Haifa and that she should go alone.

If someone is concerned about the condition of his own wife after him and gives advice as to what she should do, would he not—as the Guardian, as the Chief Protector and responsible Head of the Faith—would he not also think about the welfare and future destiny of the Faith he was called upon by 'Abdu'l-Bahá to protect and promote? The only logical conclusion is that he knew he was passing away, that he was fully conscious that he had not appointed another "ghuṣn" to succeed him as

Guardian, and that he preferred not to leave any Will and Testament. The Universal House of Justice, reflecting on this apparent dilemma, made the following pronouncement: "The fact that Shoghi Effendi did not leave a will cannot be adduced as evidence of his failure to obey Bahá'u'lláh—rather should we acknowledge that in his very silence there is a wisdom and a sign of his infallible guidance" (*Messages from the Universal House of Justice* ¶35.3).

I recall the gist of my private conversations with many friends in November 1957 when it was realized that Shoghi Effendi had unexpectedly passed away, had not appointed a successor as Guardian after him, and had left no will. We concluded that the best thing we could do was to reread more carefully 'Abdu'l-Bahá's Will and Testament as well as Shoghi Effendi's writings in order to understand more clearly the hidden implications and mysteries of these inspired documents.

I will share with you my own personal insights on what some may have regarded as a predicament in the fortunes of our beloved Faith. Shoghi Effendi had often said to Hands of the Cause of God and visiting pilgrims that his "Dispensation of Bahá'u'lláh" was like his Will and Testament. Amatu'l-Bahá, in *The Priceless Pearl*, quotes Shoghi Effendi as having indicated that "he had said all he had to say, in many ways, in the 'Dispensation'" (213). Apart from this observation, we should note that Shoghi Effendi, referring to 'Abdu'l-Bahá's Will, had written in his "Dispensation", "His Will and Testament should thus be regarded as the perpetual, the indissoluble link which the mind of Him Who is the Mystery of God has conceived in order to insure the continuity of the three ages that constitute the component parts of the Bahá'í Dispensation" (*World Order* 143–4). In the same document, Shoghi Effendi categorically stated, "The axis round which [the] institutions [of the Administrative Order] revolve are the authentic provisions of the Will and Testament of 'Abdu'l-Bahá" (156).

We should therefore consider not that we, as Bahá'ís, lived for only 36 years under the provisions of 'Abdu'l-Bahá's Will and Testament but that the worldwide Bahá'í community does now and in the future will continue to live under the provisions of that same Will for the rest of the Dispensation, as it is this document which links the Formative and Golden Ages together.

There is one other area that needs to be clarified, as, unfortunately, a slight confusion has been created in the minds of some of the friends regarding the respective areas of infallibility of the Guardianship and the Universal House of Justice. 'Abdu'l-Bahá's Will and Shoghi Effendi's "Dispensation" define the specific areas of responsibility of these two institutions, namely, that "interpretation" is exclusively confined to the Guardianship and that "legislation" is exclusively assigned to the Universal House of Justice. There is nothing in either the Will or "The Dispensation", however, which restricts the condition of infallibility to these two areas of specific responsibility. Shoghi Effendi's "Dispensation", referring to the twin institutions of the Guardianship and the Universal House of Justice, assures us, "Neither can, nor will ever, infringe upon the sacred and prescribed domain of the other" (*World Order* 150). The Will and Testament of 'Abdu'l-Bahá, referring to these two institutions, categorically states, "Whatsoever they decide is of God" (*Will and Testament* 11). This is not only broad-based but all-comprehensive.

According to the terms of this Will and Testament, the Universal House of Justice, in addition to being the legislative body, is the "body [to which] all things must be referred" (*Will and Testament* 14). It is, furthermore, the body to resolve "all the difficult problems" (14), "all problems which have caused difference" (20), and "questions that are obscure" (20). Shoghi Effendi, in his "Dispensation", assigns it the additional responsibility to "apply" (*World Order* 145) the Laws revealed by Bahá'u'lláh, conduct the "administrative affairs of the Faith"

(153), and ensure the "integrity" of the teachings (148), the "flexibility" of the Faith, and the "unity" of its followers (148).

In fact, as we have already seen from one of his early letters quoted above, Shoghi Effendi gives us this impressive view of the work of the House of Justice: "We must trust to time, and the guidance of God's Universal House of Justice, to obtain a clearer and fuller understanding of [the] provisions and implications [of the Will and Testament of 'Abdu'l-Bahá]" (*Bahá'í Administration* 62).

The Declaration of Trust and By-Laws of the National Assembly were drawn up by the National Spiritual Assembly of the United States under the direct guidance of Shoghi Effendi. Moreover, he wanted the clauses of this national constitution to be adopted by every National Spiritual Assembly. As the document includes clauses which deal with legal issues related to officially incorporated associations in every country, Shoghi Effendi stated that such secondary provisions could be changed by each National Assembly to conform to the requirements of the law current in its country. But, as the document contained basic Bahá'í principles and concepts, such fundamental provisions were to be universally adopted throughout the Bahá'í world. In this context, it is highly significant that the provisions of Article IX of the National By-Laws are as follows:

Where the National Spiritual Assembly has been given in these By-Laws exclusive and final jurisdiction, and paramount executive authority, in all matters pertaining to the activities and affairs of the Bahá'í Cause in...[the given country] it is understood that any decision made or action taken upon such matters shall be subject in every instance to ultimate review and approval by the Guardian of the Cause or the Universal House of Justice. (*Bahá'í World* 13:554)

The reason why I am quoting this particular clause, so carefully worded and approved by Shoghi Effendi, is to draw your attention to the word "or" in the last two lines. If the word had been "and" instead of "or" you can well imagine the laborious task which all incorporated National Assemblies would have faced with their respective governments in order to amend the wording of this clause.

I once again repeat that the exclusivity attached to the areas of specific responsibility of each of the twin institutions of the Guardianship and the Universal House of Justice is one thing, and the extent of infallibility attached to their respective activities on behalf of the promotion and protection of the Faith (*World Order* 20) is another thing. Unfortunately, these two separate concepts have not been kept separate in some minds, and thus some confused thinking has arisen. A moment's reflection on this point would dispel these misgivings.

Questions related:

Q. Could you comment on the Will and Testament of 'Abdu'l-Bahá as to when and under what circumstances it was written?

A. The Master's Will and Testament is in three parts. No dates are fixed on the document itself. From the context, however, we could assume that the first part must have been written during the period when the first Commission of Investigation arrived in the Holy Land, or soon after. The second section clearly must have been written in 1907, when the second Commission of Investigation was sent, because it is in this section that 'Abdu'l-Bahá says He is "in very great danger". We have no clues so far on the possible period when the third section was written.

Q. Was the first conclave of the Hands of the Cause and the appointment of nine Hands to serve in the Holy Land a fulfilment of the provision in the Will and Testament of 'Abdu'l-Bahá?

A. It does not appear to me to be so, because the nine were selected in the light of the availability of those Hands who could be in or move to the Holy Land and not through a process of election. Furthermore, the nine elected Hands of the Cause envisaged in 'Abdu'l-Bahá's Will were meant to assist Shoghi Effendi during his lifetime in his work.

Q. How was the unity of the Faith protected during the six or so years between the passing of the Guardian and the election of the Universal House of Justice?

A. The Hands, in their messages to the Bahá'í world, made it quite clear that since the entire Bahá'í world was engaged in prosecuting the objectives of the Ten Year Plan, all efforts were being exerted under the infallible guidance of Shoghi Effendi's objectives for the Crusade. After the Crusade was over, there was no choice but to establish the Universal House of Justice, so that once again the Bahá'ís of the world would labour under Divine Guidance. It is clear, therefore, that the unity of the Cause was preserved through nothing other than the power of the Covenant.

Q. If the two cases stolen by the Covenant-breakers are found, what will be the situation regarding the possible falsification of the Holy Texts by them?

A. This is of course a decision that will be taken by the Universal House of Justice if the contents of the cases are recovered. Rúḥíyyih Khánum often said that Shoghi Effendi had mentioned more than once that there can be no assurance that the texts of the documents had not been tampered with by the Covenant-breakers.

Q. What happened to the International Bahá'í Council after the passing of Shoghi Effendi in 1957?

A. The International Bahá'í Council continued to exist under the Custodians of the Faith, namely, the Hands, in the Holy Land until 1961, when there was an international election by mail by members of National Assemblies existing at the time. This election resulted in a new membership.

Q. Is the institution of the Guardianship embodied in his writings?

A. Of course we cannot say that the Guardianship, as an ongoing institution, is found in his writings. Just as the office of the Centre of the Covenant is not with us as an ongoing institution, yet we refer to 'Abdu'l-Bahá's writings for guidance, in the same way, we turn to the writings of Shoghi Effendi as interpreter of our Faith for the guidance he has shed on the purport, intent, and implications of Those Who had the reins of the Faith in Their Hands before him.

Q. I think 'Abdu'l-Bahá gave two alternatives of succession after Him, namely, a House of Justice with the Guardian and a House of Justice without him, in order to protect Shoghi Effendi after Him. Do you think 'Abdu'l-Bahá knew what would happen to Shoghi Effendi during the latter's ministry?

A. Shoghi Effendi, in his "Dispensation", states that "...in the person of 'Abdu'l-Bahá the incompatible characteristics of a human nature and superhuman knowledge and perfection have been blended and are completely harmonized" (*World Order* 134). It is obviously impossible for anyone in any discussion to take away from 'Abdu'l-Bahá's inner reality His "superhuman knowledge and perfection". In the light of this, it would be entirely in order, I think, to be confident in the conclusion that 'Abdu'l-Bahá, in His inner being, would have been aware of future events.

As to the question of using two alternatives for the future House of Justice, in light of what happened to the Aghsáns, all of whom broke the Covenant during Shoghi Effendi's lifetime, I tend to agree with you that 'Abdu'l-Bahá's purpose was to protect Shoghi Effendi.

During Shoghi Effendi's ministry, there were seven Aghsáns, all grandsons of 'Abdu'l-Bahá: two of them were his own brothers, and five of them were male first cousins. Shoghi Effendi's first reference to "future Guardians" is found in his Dispensation. At that time all the seven contemporary Aghsáns were alive and still outwardly faithful under the Covenant. He also referred to future Guardians in a letter written to an individual believer in November 1948 (*Lights of Guidance* no. 1047). At that time some Aghsáns were still within the pale of the Faith. Indeed, in a letter addressed to the friends in the East, dated Naw-Rúz 105 of the Bahá'í era, that is, some eight years before he passed away, Shoghi Effendi wrote a prayer in which he supplicates Bahá'u'lláh that those who have removed themselves from the Bahá'í Fold may have a change of heart, may compensate for what has escaped them, and may be reinstated in the Bahá'í community. As you see, he was still hoping that some of the Aghsáns would sincerely repent for their past actions—a possibility which never materialized. Of course, Shoghi Effendi had no offspring and therefore found himself, by force of circumstance, unable to appoint anyone to succeed him as Guardian in accordance with the provisions of the Will and Testament of 'Abdu'l-Bahá.

THE CONSTITUTION OF THE UNIVERSAL HOUSE OF JUSTICE

On 18 October 1927, referring to the Declaration of Trust and
By-Laws of the National Spiritual Assembly, Shoghi Effendi
wrote the following to the National Assembly of the United
States and Canada:

You can but faintly imagine how comforting a stimulant
and how helpful a guide its publication and circulation will
be to those patient and toiling workers in Eastern lands...
You can hardly realize how substantially it would
contribute to pave the way for the elaboration of the
beginnings of the constitution of the worldwide Bahá'í
Community that will form the permanent basis upon which
the blest and sanctified edifice of the first International
House of Justice will securely rest and flourish. (*Bahá'í
Administration* 143)

In a letter referring to the same subject, addressed to the Bahá'ís
in Iran, Shoghi Effendi refers to the need for the Persian National
Assembly to have its own constitution and points out that the
constitution of National Assemblies is the Greater Law of God's
Holy Faith, while the constitution of the Universal House of
Justice is its Most Great Law. In 1934, when he wrote his
"Dispensation", Shoghi Effendi once again referred to the future
constitution of the Supreme Body of the Faith.

When the Universal House of Justice was formed in 1963, it
was able to launch in April of the following year its first teaching
and consolidation Plan, which was the Nine Year Plan. One of
the goals of that Plan, set aside as an objective of the World
Centre, was to draft the Constitution governing the operation of
the House of Justice as well as the affairs of the worldwide
Bahá'í community. In view of the mounting cares and
responsibilities of the Universal House of Justice and the

45

meticulous concentration required to produce such a vitally important document, it took most of the nine years under this first Plan to bring this project to conclusion.

On 26 November 1972, the following message was sent to all National Spiritual Assemblies:

WITH GRATEFUL JOYOUS HEARTS ANNOUNCE ENTIRE BAHÁ'Í WORLD ADOPTION PROFOUNDLY SIGNIFICANT STEP IN UNFOLDMENT MISSION SUPREME ORGAN BAHÁ'Í WORLD COMMONWEALTH THROUGH FORMULATION CONSTITUTION UNIVERSAL HOUSE OF JUSTICE. AFTER OFFERING HUMBLE PRAYERS GRATITUDE ON DAY COVENANT AT THREE SACRED THRESHOLDS BAHJÍ HAIFA MEMBERS GATHERED COUNCIL CHAMBER PRECINCTS HOUSE BLESSED MASTER APPENDED THEIR SIGNATURES FIXED SEAL ON INSTRUMENT ENVISAGED WRITINGS BELOVED GUARDIAN HAILED BY HIM AS MOST GREAT LAW FAITH BAHÁ'U'LLÁH. FULLY ASSURED MEASURE JUST TAKEN WILL FURTHER REINFORCE TIES BINDING WORLD CENTER TO NATIONAL LOCAL COMMUNITIES THROUGHOUT WORLD RELEASE FRESH ENERGIES INCREASE ENTHUSIASM CONFIDENCE VALIANT WORKERS HIS DIVINE VINEYARD LABORING ASSIDUOUSLY BRING MANKIND UNDER SHELTER HIS ALL-GLORIOUS COVENANT. (*Messages from the Universal House of Justice* ¶123.3)

The Constitution of the Universal House of Justice was published as a separate document, comprising 14 pages. It was also published in *The Bahá'í World*, volume XV, pages 555 to 564. It has two sections: "The Declaration of Trust", which consists of five pages, and the "By-Laws", which consists of nine pages. The Declaration of Trust has a preamble, which is a quotation from the opening paragraphs of Bahá'u'lláh's *Epistle to the Son of the Wolf,* described by Shoghi Effendi as "the last outstanding Tablet revealed by the Pen of Bahá'u'lláh" (*God Passes By* 219).

This preamble, consisting of Bahá'u'lláh's own Words, I will quote in full:

> In the name of God, the One, the Incomparable, the All-Powerful, the All-Knowing, the All-Wise. The light that is shed from the heaven of bounty, and the benediction that shineth from the dawning-place of the will of God, the Lord of the Kingdom of Names, rest upon Him Who is the Supreme Mediator, the Most Exalted Pen, Him Whom God hath made the dawning-place of His most excellent names and the dayspring of His most exalted attributes. Through Him the light of unity hath shone forth above the horizon of the world, and the law of oneness hath been revealed amidst the nations, who, with radiant faces, have turned towards the Supreme Horizon, and acknowledged that which the Tongue of Utterance hath spoken in the Kingdom of His knowledge: "Earth and heaven, glory and dominion, are God's, the Omnipotent, the Almighty, the Lord of grace abounding!" (*Epistle* 1–2)

It is significant that in this passage, Bahá'u'lláh refers to "the light of unity [that] hath shone forth above the horizon of the world, and the law of oneness [that] hath been revealed amidst the nations". Likewise, the reference in the last sentence to "earth and heaven" as belonging to God is also significant when we recall the words in the Revelation of St John, which I have already quoted, giving the promise that a new earth and a new heaven will be manifested. The "earth", beyond any doubt, refers to the earthly civilization that the Cause of God is destined to establish, and the "heaven" mentioned by Bahá'u'lláh in this passage is undoubtedly the heaven of His new Revelation.

After this potent introductory passage, revealed by Bahá'u'lláh and so appropriate as an opening statement to His Most Great Law, the Universal House of Justice expresses its elation and gratitude with the following sentence: "With joyous and thankful hearts we testify to the abundance of God's Mercy, to the perfection of His Justice and to the fulfilment of His Ancient Promise" (*Constitution* 1).

The next paragraph is of 17 lines, in which the following points are solemnly and explicitly made:

1. The Station of Bahá'u'lláh is clearly defined as described in titles given to Him by Shoghi Effendi in *God Passes By*, pages 93 to 94, such as "the Fountain of the Most Great Justice", "the Creator of a new World Order", "the Inspirer and Founder of a world civilization", "the Judge", "the Lawgiver", and "the Unifier" and "Redeemer of all mankind".
2. The next point is a reference to Bahá'u'lláh's Covenant and the vital function it performed after His Ascension by canalizing the forces revealed by the Revelation of Bahá'u'lláh throughout the Heroic and Formative Ages of the Faith.
3. The Universal House of Justice is then specifically mentioned as one of the two successors of Bahá'u'lláh and 'Abdu'l-Bahá under that same Covenant, and the responsibility ordained for it is to "safeguard the unity" of the followers of the Faith and to "maintain the integrity and flexibility of its teachings", as clearly stipulated by Shoghi Effendi in his "Dispensation" (*World Order* 148).

The next paragraph is a passage extracted from the Tablet known as "Lawḥ-i-Maqṣúd", revealed in 'Akká and described by Shoghi Effendi as one of the Tablets revealed by Him as His

Mission drew to a close and which contains "precepts and principles which lie at the very core of His Faith" (*God Passes By* 216). This passage is highly relevant, as it defines the "fundamental purpose animating the Faith of God and His Religion" (*Tablets of Bahá'u'lláh* 168). In Bahá'u'lláh's words, this purpose is "to safeguard the interests and promote the unity of the human race" and "to foster the spirit of love and fellowship amongst men". In the same passage He describes His Faith as "the straight Path" and His new World Order as "the fixed and immovable foundation" whose "strength" can never be "impaired" nor its structure "undermined" by the "changes and chances of the world" and the "revolution of countless centuries" (168).

The next paragraph is a quotation from 'Abdu'l-Bahá's Will and Testament, in which the sphere of responsibility of the House of Justice is defined, namely, to decide on "all that is not expressly recorded" in the Most Holy Book and to be the Body to which "every one must turn".

The following paragraph clearly determines what constitutes "the binding terms of reference of the Universal House of Justice", "its bedrock foundation". These have been identified as "the revealed Word of Bahá'u'lláh" and "the interpretations and expositions" recorded by 'Abdu'l-Bahá and Shoghi Effendi as Interpreters of the Revealed Word. This sentence clearly specifies that Shoghi Effendi is, after 'Abdu'l-Bahá, "the sole authority in the interpretation of Bahá'í Scripture". This sentence further confirms the refusal of the House of Justice to engage in interpretation of the Writings.

The last sentence of this paragraph is extremely weighty, as it categorically states, "The authority of these Texts is absolute and immutable until such time as Almighty God shall reveal His new Manifestation, to Whom will belong all authority and power."

The paragraph that follows calls to mind the passing of Shoghi Effendi without his having appointed a Guardian of the Cause to succeed him. In view of this circumstance, the

Universal House of Justice declares that it is now the "Head of the Faith and its supreme institution".

Therefore, the coordination of the work of the Hands of the Cause, the extension into the future of their functions of protection and propagation, and the receipt and disbursement of the Ḥuqúqu'lláh would, of necessity, devolve upon the Universal House of Justice.

A word of explanation about the offering and receipt of the Ḥuqúqu'lláh would, I feel, be appropriate. The Law of the Ḥuqúq was revealed by Bahá'u'lláh in the Kitáb-i-Aqdas in paragraph 97. In this verse, Bahá'u'lláh stipulates that the Ḥuqúq belongs to God and has "to be rendered unto Him". Nowhere in the Aqdas, or in His other Writings, does Bahá'u'lláh explicitly specify who should be the recipient of this offering after His Ascension. It was clear, however, that whoever was specified as Bahá'u'lláh's Successor, namely, 'Abdu'l-Bahá, the Centre of the Covenant to Whom all must turn, would be, beyond any doubt, the recipient of such payments. In His Will and Testament, 'Abdu'l-Bahá provides for this money offering to be paid "through the Guardian of the Cause of God" (*Will and Testament* 15). This was so because Shoghi Effendi was the institution to whom all were to turn after the passing of 'Abdu'l-Bahá.

Following the same pattern, the Universal House of Justice, in its capacity as Successor not only to Shoghi Effendi but also to 'Abdu'l-Bahá and Bahá'u'lláh, found logically and correctly that it was the institution destined to receive and expend the Ḥuqúqu'lláh, in accordance with the spirit and purpose of this Fund as clearly enunciated in 'Abdu'l-Bahá's Will and Testament, namely, "the diffusion of the Fragrances of God and the exaltation of His Word, for benevolent pursuits and for the common weal" (*Will and Testament* 15). In the light of these circumstances, the following Words of Bahá'u'lláh acquire added significance: "There is a prescribed ruling for the Ḥuqúqu'lláh. After the House of Justice hath come into being, the law thereof will be made manifest, in conformity with the Will of God" (*Right of God* no. 59).

So far, we have looked at the contents of the first six paragraphs of the text of the Constitution. These six paragraphs are followed by five sections which are described as "powers and duties with which the Universal House of Justice has been invested". I must explain here that the Universal House of Justice commissioned its Research Department to compile and present to it each and every statement made in the original texts of Bahá'u'lláh, 'Abdu'l-Bahá, and Shoghi Effendi on the subject of the Universal House of Justice, its powers, and its duties. Many of these texts had already been translated into English or, as in the case of the writings of Shoghi Effendi, were already available in English. However, a great deal had to be translated and supplied to the House of Justice for its consideration. The contents of these five sections are all, without any exception, based on these texts. I hope that it will not be in the too distant future when students and scholars of the Faith are able to identify the powers and duties tabulated in these sections and to find their roots in the Writings of Bahá'u'lláh and the interpretive expositions made by 'Abdu'l-Bahá and Shoghi Effendi.

It is beyond the scope of my presentation to provide you with a list of references showing the source of each of the functions of the Supreme Body as set forth in these five sections. However, I will refer to each section separately and will give you my commentary on any aspect which may need some clarification.

Section one: "To ensure the preservation of the Sacred Texts and to safeguard their inviolability; to analyse, classify, and coordinate the Writings; and to defend and protect the Cause of God and emancipate it from the fetters of repression and persecution" (*Constitution* 5). The preservation of the Sacred Texts is clearly a primary responsibility of the Head of the Faith. This is why Shoghi Effendi constructed the International Archives Building and the Universal House of Justice later added an extension to that edifice, in order to provide the latest scientific facilities available to preserve papers, documents, and artefacts. The word "inviolability", used in this connection, refers to the need to protect the Sacred Texts from any physical harm as well as uphold the sacredness of the Holy Writings and preserve their integrity.

The duty to analyse, classify, and coordinate the Writings is currently being discharged by the Research Department for and on behalf of the Universal House of Justice. These functions presently have their home in the edifice around the Arc that is known to the friends as the Centre for the Study of the Texts.

The duty of defending and protecting the Cause of God is clearly implicit in the Words of Bahá'u'lláh calling on the men of the House of Justice in the Kitáb-i-Aqdas: "O ye Men of Justice! Be ye, in the realm of God, shepherds unto His sheep and guard them... even as ye would guard your own sons" (Aqdas ¶52). This section ends with the statement that the House of Justice is vested with the responsibility of emancipating the Faith "from the fetters of repression and persecution". The second stage in the evolution of the Faith is its emancipation from the fetters of repression. This emancipation will take place when the religious authorities in a given country pronounce and regard the laws and principles of the Faith as separate from and alien to the official established religion of that country. The steps taken by National Spiritual Assemblies throughout the world and the Bahá'í International Community (with its seat in New York)—all functioning under the direction of the Universal House of Justice—have succeeded in protecting the Persian Bahá'í community from the professed intention of the Iranian government to destroy the Cause of God, root and branch, in Bahá'u'lláh's native land. It is hoped of course that these efforts will eventually lead to the emancipation of the Persian Bahá'í community from the clutches of a traditional enemy, which has sought to strangulate it ever since its inception 16 decades ago.

Section two: This entire section deals with the obligations of the Universal House of Justice in the three fields of proclamation, expansion, and consolidation. A partial and initial implementation of the provisions in this section can be seen through the release of the *Synopsis and Codification of the Kitáb-i-Aqdas* and, subsequently, the translation into English of the entire Kitáb-i-Aqdas, supported by copious annotations; the dissemination of newly translated texts from the Writings of Bahá'u'lláh, the Báb, and 'Abdu'l-Bahá; and, more particularly, the publication of the book *The Proclamation of Bahá'u'lláh* as well as its two open letters to the peoples of the world and to religious leaders, respectively.

The reference in this section to the promotion of the spiritual qualities that must characterize individual and collective Bahá'í life is best exemplified by the importance attached to teaching institutes, study circles, devotional meetings, children's classes, and the division of each home front into clusters, as called for under the current Plan. As to the last part of this section, regarding cordiality and peace among the nations and the advancement and betterment of the world, these objectives are, for the time being, being spearheaded on the international level by our Bahá'í International Community offices in New York, Geneva, and selected capitals in Europe.

Section three: The next section deals with the vital responsibilities of the House of Justice as the highest legislative body of the Faith and the institution to which all must turn for the solution of problems that have caused differences among the friends and for the elucidation of questions that are obscure. As I have already noted, these functions are embedded in the Writings of Bahá'u'lláh and in the provisions of the Will and Testament of 'Abdu'l-Bahá.

The latter part of the section begins with the duty incumbent upon the House of Justice to safeguard the rights, freedom, and initiative of individuals. This opens the way for individuals, if they feel that their essential rights have been trampled upon by decisions of institutions on the local or national level within a given country, to appeal to the Universal House of Justice for redress of grievances.

The last clause of this section deals with the development of countries and the stability of states. These functions can be discharged effectively by the Universal House of Justice when the World Order of Bahá'u'lláh has been ushered in, the Faith universally acknowledged, and the Universal House of Justice, as the Supreme Organ of that Order, recognized among the nations.

Section four: The fourth section is a pronouncement on the duty of the House of Justice to apply the Laws of the Faith as they progressively become binding (as happened in the case of the Law of Ḥuqúqu'lláh and the ordinances related to obligatory prayers and fasting) and to uphold the ideal of rectitude of conduct which, as Shoghi Effendi has written, has "implications of justice, equity, truthfulness, honesty, fair-mindedness, reliability, and trustworthiness"—standards that must distinguish "every phase of the life of the Bahá'í community" (*Advent* 23).

This section addresses the development of the Spiritual and Administrative Centre of the Bahá'í Faith in the Holy Land. The establishment of the International Teaching Centre following the appointment of Boards of Counsellors, as well as the addition of assistants to Auxiliary Board members, the erection of new buildings round the Arc, the extension of the gardens in Bahjí, the construction of the Terraces surrounding the Shrine of the Báb, and the establishment of two new pilgrim houses in Bahjí and Haifa are among some of the more obvious developments that have taken place at the World Centre during the past four decades.

There is included in this section a very interesting function of the House of Justice. It is to ensure that no institution within the Cause may abuse its privileges nor decline in the exercise of its rights and prerogatives. This function of the House of Justice requires both vigilant alertness and appropriate intervention when the vital interests of the Faith are disregarded. The final part of this section deals with the administration of the funds and properties of the Faith, a function which does not need any amplification.

Section five: The last section deals with the judiciary powers of the Universal House of Justice in adjudicating disputes, settling differences, enforcing decisions, and applying sanctions. Finally, as a crowning obligation, the House's judiciary responsibilities are summed up with these challenging words: "to be the exponent and guardian of that Divine Justice which can alone ensure the security of, and establish the reign of law and order in, the world" (*Constitution* 6). This ends the five sections outlining the duties and powers of the Universal House of Justice.

The legislative powers stipulated above will remain vested permanently in the Universal House of Justice. However, none of the provisions prevent the Universal House of Justice from making it possible for separate institutions to be established on the international level to assume the executive and judicial responsibilities now discharged by the House of Justice itself.

The paragraph which follows introduces a quotation from Shoghi Effendi's "The Dispensation of Bahá'u'lláh". In this paragraph three titles for the members of the House of Justice are given, namely, "the Men of Justice", "the people of Bahá who have been mentioned in the Book of Names", and the "Trustees of God" who are "dayprings of authority". The title "Men of Justice" is taken from the Kitáb-i-Aqdas, paragraph 52. The title "people of Bahá who have been mentioned in the Book of Names" is taken from the Tablet of Carmel (*Gleanings* 16). The title "Trustees of God" who are "dayprings of authority" is taken from the Tablet of Bahá'u'lláh known as "The Glad-Tidings". The passage appears in the Thirteenth "Glad-Tidings". It is under the same Thirteenth "Glad-Tidings" that Bahá'u'lláh says, "All matters of State should be referred to the House of Justice..." It is likewise in this same passage of "The Glad-Tidings" that Bahá'u'lláh states, "that which traineth the world is justice, for it is upheld by two pillars, reward and punishment".

Finally, it is in this same section that Bahá'u'lláh refers to the members of the House of Justice as "the recipients of divine inspiration from the unseen kingdom" (*Tablets of Bahá'u'lláh* 27).

Regarding the specific designation of "the people of Baha" as revealed in the Tablet of Carmel, many friends have asked what the "Book of Names" is, in which mention is made of these Trustees (*Tablets of Bahá'u'lláh* 5). There is a Tablet revealed by the Báb known as "The Book of Names", but no such reference is found in that document. I will share with you my own understanding of this reference. The word "Names" in the original is "Asmá". This word has been translated by Shoghi Effendi sometimes as "Names" and at other times as "Titles", depending on the context. The first sense would denote divine and heavenly qualities and attributes, as in such phrases as "God's Most Excellent Names". In the latter sense, i.e. "Titles", it could apply to appellations or accolades bestowed on an individual as a sign of praise or rank. In the Bahá'í Writings we find such titles as "Centre of the Covenant", "Guardian of the Cause of God", "Hands of the Cause of God", "Houses of Justice", "Trustees of the Merciful", "Knights of Bahá'u'lláh", etc. Thus, the "Book of Names" could be God's Mystical Book in which are recorded the titles and accolades bestowed on His ministers, as well as on promoters, protectors, and/or defenders of His Cause, either individually or as a collective group.

As to the quotation from "The Dispensation of Bahá'u'lláh" that begins with the words "In the conduct of the administrative affairs..." (*Constitution* 6), three important points have been incorporated by Shoghi Effendi in this passage. The first is that the members of the Universal House of Justice should be governed in the discharge of their functions by the prayerful promptings of their conscience and not by the feelings or convictions of those who directly or indirectly elect them; which clearly implies, thereby, that they are responsible before God and not to those whom they represent. This is a clear negation of one of the essential features of a democratic system. All democracies make the elected responsible to the electorate. This is why referendums are resorted to in democratic systems of government, in order to determine what the popular vote will decide on a given issue.

The second point is that they must acquaint themselves with the conditions prevailing in the community. This duty counterbalances referendums and is a provision incorporated in the system of Bahá'í Administration in order to offset the withdrawal of authority from the mass of the electorate. Obviously the members of the House of Justice have the obligation individually to be alert to the general sentiments and opinions of the community and institutionally to depend on faithful and sympathetic agencies, such as the Counsellors, to share with them the trends of thought and feeling among the rank and file of the believers.

The third point is the quotation from the Writings of Bahá'u'lláh giving the assurance that "God will verily inspire them with whatsoever He willeth." This is followed by Shoghi Effendi's explanation that the elected members—and I am stressing the word "elected" in this passage—are "the recipients of the divine guidance which is at once the life-blood and ultimate safeguard of this Revelation".

Shoghi Effendi was appointed by 'Abdu'l-Bahá to be the Head and a member of the Universal House of Justice. He was not an elected member of the Supreme Body. Shoghi Effendi, as interpreter of the Teachings, is assuring us here that the elected members are recipients of the promised divine guidance.

The last paragraph of the Declaration of Trust states the date on which the Universal House of Justice was first elected, in accordance with the provisions of the Will and Testament of 'Abdu'l-Bahá and in response to the call of the Hands of the Cause of God, who were described by Shoghi Effendi as "the Chief Stewards of Bahá'u'lláh's embryonic World Commonwealth" (*Constitution* 6).

This paragraph also quotes two titles given by Shoghi Effendi to the Universal House of Justice, namely, the "crowning glory" of the administrative institutions of Bahá'u'lláh and the "nucleus and forerunner" of His World Order.

Following this paragraph is a space where the nine members who were in office on 26 November 1972, namely, the Day of the Covenant, have signed their names in alphabetical order. The last paragraph gives the date of the document and states that it was signed in the city of Haifa. The last feature of the document is the impression of the seal of the Universal House of Justice.

Annexed to the Declaration of Trust is the nine-page document containing the By-Laws of the Constitution. The preamble to the By-Laws is followed by 11 main clauses, as follows:

I.	Membership in the Bahá'í Community
II.	Local Spiritual Assemblies
III.	National Spiritual Assemblies
IV.	Obligations of Members of Spiritual Assemblies
V.	The Universal House of Justice [consisting of six sub-clauses]
VI.	Bahá'í Elections
VII.	The Right of Review
VIII.	Appeals
IX.	The Boards of Counsellors
X.	The Auxiliary Boards
XI.	Amendment

Some of these clauses which deal with general issues, such as membership in the community, Local and National Assemblies and their obligations, and the methods of Bahá'í elections and appeals, I will not go into, as they are matters of common knowledge and experience for Bahá'ís in every land. I will confine my comments to those clauses which deal directly with the work and sphere of authority of the Universal House of Justice. We will first deal with the brief preamble, which gives a concise and complete definition of the Administrative Order as it is operating in the Bahá'í World at this time. The first paragraph refers to the House of Justice as the "supreme institution of the Administrative Order" (*Constitution* 8). This Order, the preamble states, consists of two parts: (1) Elected Councils on local, national, and international levels that are invested with all three powers, namely, legislative, executive, and judicial, and (2) Individual believers appointed for the specific tasks of protecting and propagating the Faith.

The second paragraph defines the relationship of the Administrative Order to the World Order, the former being the nucleus and pattern of the latter. This Administrative Order is described as both divinely propelled and organically expanding. This development will be realized through the establishment of auxiliary and subordinate agencies, as well as by the multiplication and diversification of Bahá'í functions—all designed to promote the progress of the human race.

We have to pass over the first four clauses, as indicated earlier, and deal with clause V, which, as mentioned, has six sub-clauses. The introduction to this clause states that the membership of the Body consists of "nine men" elected from the worldwide Bahá'í community. These members are elected by the members of all National Spiritual Assemblies throughout the world. Every male adult Bahá'í in good standing throughout the world is eligible for election. It is well known to Bahá'ís that in the future the number could exceed nine, as stated in the Kitáb-i-Aqdas, "should it exceed this number it doth not matter" (¶30).

The question is often asked, "Why it is that the membership of the Supreme Body is confined to men?" In my experience the wisest way to answer this query is to quote 'Abdu'l-Bahá: "The House of Justice,... according to the explicit text of the Law of God, is confined to men; this for a wisdom of the Lord God's, which will erelong be made manifest as clearly as the sun at high noon" (*Selections from the Writings of 'Abdu'l-Bahá* 80). This statement by the Master closes the door to speculation and argumentation. I think what 'Abdu'l-Bahá means is that neither humanity nor the Bahá'í community has reached its stage of maturity. At such a stage, the age of wise judgement and well-balanced discretion would be reached by this fast-evolving world, and it would then become crystal clear as to why Bahá'u'lláh included this provision in His code of laws.

As I said earlier, this clause has six sub-clauses, and most of the sub-clauses are divided into subsidiary sections. The first sub-clause has nine subsections, from (a) to (i). The important points in these subsections are as follows:

1. The election of the Universal House of Justice is held every five years unless otherwise decided by the Supreme Body. At such a time, the elected members shall continue in their office until their successors are elected and can have their first meeting.

2. The principal business of the International Convention is the election of the House of Justice members, the deliberation on the affairs of the Cause, and the submission of recommendations for consideration by the Universal House of Justice.

3. If, at the time of the election, the House of Justice considers it impractical or unwise to hold the Convention, it shall determine how the election should take place. Based on this, the House of Justice decided not to hold an International Convention in 2003—the first time it has made such a decision since being formed—and instructed members of National Spiritual Assemblies to cast their ballots by mail, since it was considered impractical and unwise to hold a convention in view of the high insecurity prevailing in the country and the grave dangers

involved in international travelling during the month of April 2003.

4. If a member of a National Assembly who has cast his ballot by mail subsequently ceases to be a member of the Assembly, his ballot shall remain valid unless, in the meantime, a successor has been elected and the ballot of the latter has been received in Haifa.

5. In case of a tie vote or votes, additional balloting will be held for the persons tied. As National Conventions are held on a date soon after the Riḍván period in the years when the International Convention is convened, the electors in such a case would be the newly elected members of the National Assembly.

The second sub-clause deals with vacancies in the membership of the Universal House of Justice. Four possibilities are envisaged: (1) Death of a member, (2) Dismissal of a member by the House of Justice if he has committed a sin injurious to the common weal, (3) Removal of a member from membership if the House of Justice considers him to be unable to fulfil his functions, and (4) Relinquishment of membership by a member, with the approval of the House of Justice. The first and fourth possibilities have occurred in the past, but the second and third have not yet happened, and let us hope that they will never need to be implemented.

The next sub-clause deals with by-elections. If a vacancy occurs between two International Conventions, the voters shall be the members of the National Assemblies in office. If, in the judgement of the Universal House of Justice, the date falls too close to the date of the regular International Convention, it would not proceed with the by-election. In such cases, the Universal House of Justice would function with, say, only eight members.

The next subsection lays down procedures for the first meeting of the House of Justice after election and clearly stipulates that the House of Justice has no officers and that its meetings are therefore conducted in a manner decided by the House of Justice itself. It is common knowledge that at this time in the evolution of the work of the House of Justice, the chairmanship rotates among the members in alphabetical order on a weekly basis.

This sub-clause provides for quorums of less than the full membership for specific classes of business. It enables members of the House to take annual leave or at periods they may wish to determine without hampering the day-to-day work of the Supreme Body. This does not prevent the Universal House of Justice from contacting absent members by phone or otherwise for their input on issues under consideration.

The last two sub-clauses deal with the signature on letters written by the Universal House of Justice itself, in either English or Persian, and the need in each case to affix the Seal of the Supreme Body. The Universal House of Justice also lays down specific methods for recording its own decisions.

The next section, which is unique to the work of the House of Justice, is clause VII, entitled "The Right of Review". This clause is in two parts, the first part being an extension of a similar article found in all national constitutions giving the right to the Head of the Faith to modify or even reverse decisions or actions taken by subsidiary agencies of the Administrative Order. The second part anticipates the possibility of a Spiritual Assembly, either National or Local, failing to take action or reach a decision on an issue which, in the judgement of the Universal House of Justice, is vital to the interests of the Faith and calls for specific action to be taken. In such cases, the House of Justice gives itself the right to take action directly on the matter.

We will now deal with the last three clauses of the By-Laws, namely, section IX, The Boards of Counsellors; section X, The Auxiliary Boards; and section XI, Amendment. Section IX provides for the appointment by the House of Justice of individual Bahá'ís who can be entrusted with the functions of protection and propagation of the Faith, as assigned to the Hands of the Cause of God in accordance with the Will and Testament of 'Abdu'l-Bahá. Each Counsellor is expected to carry out his duties within the zone where he resides. Terms of office are determined by the House of Justice. The current term is five years. This clause further stipulates that the work of a Counsellor renders him ineligible for service on Local or National administrative bodies. If he is elected to the Universal House of Justice, he obviously has to relinquish his status as a Counsellor.

Section X defines the functions of Auxiliary Board members as deputies, assistants, and advisors to the Counsellors. Each Auxiliary Board member is allotted a specific area in which to serve. An Auxiliary Board member, unlike a Counsellor, is eligible for any elective office. If elected, he must decide whether to remain on the Board or accept the elective post. Similarly, if elected to the Universal House of Justice, he automatically relinquishes his status as an Auxiliary Board member. The current term for Auxiliary Board members is also five years.

Furthermore, as indicated by Shoghi Effendi, there are two Boards, one for the protection and one for the propagation of the Faith. The number of Auxiliary Boards for each continent is decided by the Universal House of Justice. The Counsellors, in their turn, divide this number throughout their area of responsibility, as the need in each area demands.

The last clause stipulates that all amendments may be made only when the full membership of the House of Justice is present. The Constitution of the House of Justice in its present form has not yet been amended. However, two important decisions affecting the Boards of Counsellors and Auxiliary Boards have already been taken by the House of Justice which, with the passing of time, will undoubtedly be incorporated in the Constitution as amendments to its clauses. One is the establishment of the International Teaching Centre in the Holy Land, and the other is the permission given to Auxiliary Board members to appoint assistants. These provisions do not appear in the present Constitution, since the decisions were adopted after the formulation of the Constitution in November 1972.

Questions related:

Q. Are the three functions of the House of Justice—legislative, executive, and judicial—set down in the Writings?

A. In "The Unfoldment of World Civilization" (*World Order* 203), Shoghi Effendi describes the principal institutions of the Bahá'í World Commonwealth as the "world legislature", the "world executive", and the "world tribunal".

In a statement entitled "A Procedure for the Conduct of a Local Spiritual Assembly", which was published in every volume of *The Bahá'í World* during the lifetime of Shoghi Effendi, we find reference to the three separate powers of every Spiritual Assembly. For example, in Volume 12 (the last volume published in the lifetime of Shoghi Effendi), page 297, we find the statement in question.

Q. Will the Universal House of Justice recognize the future Manifestation of God?

A. I have not seen anything in the Writings on this subject. However, when a pilgrim asked Shoghi Effendi this very question he said that the Universal House of Justice will surely recognize the new Manifestation of God and introduce Him to the community. Whether or not the rank and file will accept Him is a matter of speculation, and I do not wish to go into this area.

Q. According to what criteria does the Universal House of Justice decide on the length of teaching plans?

A. Obviously the House of Justice takes into consideration a variety of factors, such as the strengths and weaknesses of the Bahá'í community, the trends in world developments, and the possibilities of the future as the Faith moves towards its destiny.

Q. What is the precise difference, as stated in the Constitution, between elucidation and interpretation? How can we be sure that we are not interpreting the Writings when we deepen?

A. Shoghi Effendi had two main objectives animating his ministry: the establishment of the Universal House of Justice and the systematic launching of the provisions of the Tablets of the Divine Plan. He was endowed with a gift of knowing the mind of Bahá'u'lláh and of 'Abdu'l-Bahá. Indeed, I think he gives us a definition of "interpretation" in "The Dispensation of Bahá'u'lláh", in which he clearly states that "the Guardian has been specifically endowed with such power as he may need to reveal the purport and disclose the implications of the utterances of Bahá'u'lláh and of 'Abdu'l-Bahá" (*World Order* 151). This is a gift bestowed upon the Guardian and on 'Abdu'l-Bahá before him because they both knew and were able to disclose the nature and scope of the vision inherent in God's holy Faith.

As to "elucidation", we have already seen how Shoghi Effendi says that the Will and Testament of 'Abdu'l-Bahá conceals mysteries which would be unveiled gradually after the election of the Universal House of Justice. The letters of the House of Justice published in the volume of its messages on the question of the Guardianship and the Universal House of Justice can well be regarded as elucidations. Another instance would be the reference in the Will and Testament of 'Abdu'l-Bahá, as well as in other utterances of His, to the World Tribunal. In one of his letters to the American National Assembly, Shoghi Effendi stated,

Touching the point raised in the Secretary's letter regarding the nature and scope of the Universal Court of Arbitration, this and other similar matters will have to be explained and elucidated by the Universal House of

Justice, to which, according to the Master's explicit instructions, all important and fundamental questions must be referred. (*Bahá'í Administration* 47)

There are a number of questions that would normally come to mind about such a universal court or tribunal. Who will elect or appoint it? Will it have a term of office? Will women as well as men be eligible for membership? What will be its relationship to the Universal House of Justice? These are unsettled and obscure matters, and the Will and Testament has clearly stated that "all the difficult problems" (*Will and Testament* 14) as well as "all problems which have caused difference" (20) and "questions that are obscure" (20) will be resolved through legislation on the part of the Universal House of Justice.

Regarding study circles or deepening courses and the interpretation given by individual participants, this is a completely different situation. In such discussions, we are not only permitted to offer our understanding of the texts but are encouraged to do so. What is prohibited in the Cause is for an individual or group of individuals to offer interpretations, claim that they are authoritative, and engage in promoting such opinions among the friends. The use of our mental faculties in trying to understand a sacred text is a healthy exercise.

Q. Compared to other institutions of which you have been a member, did you feel a difference in the consultations of the Universal House of Justice?

A. I do not recall anyone asking me this question before. I have already quoted the verse in the Kitáb-i-Aqdas in which He comments about the attitude of the members of Local Spiritual Assemblies. As you recall, Bahá'u'lláh says, "They should consider themselves as entering the Court of the presence of God, the Exalted, the Most High, and as beholding Him Who is the Unseen" (¶30). Being aware of the presence of the Blessed

Beauty in the Council Chamber of a Spiritual Assembly and of the Universal House of Justice is a spiritual obligation placed on the shoulders of the elected members. It is true, however, that entering the Council Chamber of the Universal House of Justice and being privileged to participate in its consultations enables the member to become more intensely aware of the Presence of the Spirit of the Founder of our Faith. How wonderful it will be when an ever-increasing number of Local and National Spiritual Assemblies attain that degree of spiritual consciousness that enables its members to follow the exhortation of Bahá'u'lláh in His Most Holy Book. When consultations are held in such an atmosphere, Divine confirmations and guidance are sure to surround the deliberations of the members and the actions taken by the Assembly. In one of His Tablets, after enumerating the spiritual obligations of the members of consulting councils, 'Abdu'l-Bahá says, "Should they endeavour to fulfil these conditions the Grace of the Holy Spirit shall be vouchsafed unto them, and that Assembly shall become the center of the Divine blessings, the hosts of Divine confirmation shall come to their aid, and they shall day by day receive a new effusion of Spirit" (*Bahá'í Administration* 22–3).

Q. Does the House of Justice refer to the Bayán as well as the Writings of Bahá'u'lláh?

A. One of the buildings around the Arc is the edifice for the Centre for the Study of the Texts. The Research Department of the Universal House of Justice has its offices in that building. This Department specializes in providing the Universal House of Justice with texts which bear directly or indirectly on subjects that the House of Justice feels it needs in addressing an issue of legislation or one bordering on legislation. The Research Department also provides the House of Justice with extracts from the Writings of past religions, including that of the Báb, as may be needed.

The work of the House of Justice can also relate to matters that are secular or scientific in character, calling for knowledge of various fields. Such data and information is usually beyond the scope of the Research Department and is referred to another institution, which will, in the years to come, be built around the Arc. It is because of this need that the Universal House of Justice, in a letter to the Bahá'í world dated 31 August 1987, states the following in describing the immediate and future responsibilities of the International Bahá'í Library:

> This Library is the central depository of all literature published on the Faith, and is an essential source of information for the institutions of the World Centre on all subjects relating to the Cause of God and the conditions of mankind. In future decades its functions must grow, it will serve as an active center for knowledge in all fields, and it will become the kernel of great institutions of scientific investigation and discovery. (*Wider Horizon* 52)

The International Library is currently housed in the Centre for the Study of the Texts, but in the future it will have its own separate building, facing the International Archives.

With the above in mind we can visualize the Universal House of Justice in the centre of the Arc buildings. On its left is the Centre for the Study of the Texts, which provides it with information on religious scripture. On the right it is flanked by an institution which provides it with information on scientific and secular fields of knowledge. Thus, on the Mountain of God, we see the union of religion and science serving the Supreme Body of the Faith.

Q. Are the Boards of Counsellors a different institution from the Hands of the Cause?

A. According to the Master's Will and Testament, the Hands of the Cause are appointed by the Guardian. No term of office was stipulated by 'Abdu'l-Bahá, and therefore those nominated continued in office for the rest of their lives, as happened in the case of Hands of the Cause appointed by Bahá'u'lláh. The Counsellors are appointed by the Universal House of Justice for a term of five years.

Furthermore, the Hands of the Cause were due to elect from among their number nine who would give their assent to the choice of a successor to the Guardian. Such an authority has not been vested in the institution of the Counsellors.

A third distinction is that, according to the terms of 'Abdu'l-Bahá's Will, the Hands of the Cause were empowered to expel anyone opposing the Guardian, even if that person had the rank of Hand of the Cause. This provision in the Will and Testament was put into effect by the Hands when it was necessary to expel Mason Remey because of his claim to the Guardianship. Such authority of expulsion has not been given to the institution of the Counsellors.

Q. How often does the House of Justice meet? Why are decisions of the House of Justice recorded?

A. At this time, the House of Justice meets three days a week and, depending on its agenda, for the whole day. This pattern may change in the future, as there is no text on this matter. Obviously all decisions of the House of Justice have to have some documentation. The method of recording such decisions can of course change from time to time.

Q. With regard to vacancies in the membership of the Universal House of Justice, what might "a sin injurious to the common weal" be?

A. This phrase is taken from the Will and Testament of 'Abdu'l-Bahá. It is left to the Universal House of Justice to determine whether misbehaviour or misconduct of one of its members is of a magnitude that would cause harm to the well-being of the Faith. Naturally, each case will be considered separately, and, as far as I am aware, no specific definition has been given by the House of Justice on this issue.

Q. The Universal House of Justice has no officers. What are "officers" in this context?

A. This term is with reference to the by-laws of National and Local Spiritual Assemblies, and the intent is clearly the usual officers of Bahá'í consultative bodies, namely, chairman, vice-chairman, secretary, and treasurer. The Universal House of Justice has no chairman, and the office of chairmanship rotates among the members on a weekly basis in alphabetical order. The work of the secretary and treasurer is so vast and complex that special departments have been established to carry out the duties related to these functions. These departments operate under separate Policy Committees composed of House of Justice members who direct and supervise the work of these departments. It should be pointed out in this connection that all matters not specified in the Constitution of the Universal House of Justice are usually matters of detail and can be changed from time to time by the House of Justice itself, as needs arise.

Q. How shall we understand the concept of "infallibility"?

A. Bahá'u'lláh, in the Tablet of Ishráqát, explains that infallibility has "divers stations" (*Tablets of Bahá'u'lláh* 108). In *Some Answered Questions*, chapter 45, 'Abdu'l-Bahá explains that there are two kinds of infallibility, "essential" and "acquired". The essential kind is one of the distinctive powers of the Manifestation of God, and no one is given a share in this distinction. Acquired infallibility is conferred upon those who do not essentially possess the Divine Light but receive this light indirectly from its Source. 'Abdu'l-Bahá says in this chapter that such souls are "mediators of grace between God and men". He goes on to say, "If God did not protect them from error, their error would cause believing souls to fall into error, and thus the foundation of the Religion of God would be overturned, which would not be fitting nor worthy of God."

In the same chapter, 'Abdu'l-Bahá gives two examples of acquired infallibility. For the Bahá'í Faith, He mentions the institution of the Universal House of Justice, whose decisions are "under the protection and the unerring guidance of God". The other example given by 'Abdu'l-Bahá, from the Christian Dispensation, is Christ, who was the source of God's "command" and possessed the Most Great Infallibility, and His disciples, who were under His shadow and on whom He conferred His special grace. It is interesting in this connection to note that the disciples of Christ and the Imáms of the Muḥammadan Faith are mentioned as belonging to one and the same category in their respective Dispensations (*Some Answered Questions* 45–61).

It is worth noting that the authority bestowed on the disciples of Christ, as recorded in the New Testament, is expressed in the following words from Christ to His disciples: "Verily I say unto you. Whatsoever ye shall bind on earth shall be bound in heaven, and whatsoever ye shall loose on earth shall be loosed in heaven" (Matthew 18:18).

I suppose there are many other ways to understand the concept of infallibility in the Cause, but what I have shared with you is my own simple and inadequate understanding of this subject. I suppose that in the future this all-important theme will be explored more fully by the scholars of the Faith and perhaps further elucidated by the Universal House of Justice itself, if it feels it necessary to do so.

I should begin this section by recalling some of the words of Bahá'u'lláh regarding the newness and freshness of His Revelation. A few extracts will satisfy our purpose. We read, for example,

> Through the movement of Our Pen of glory We have, at the bidding of the omnipotent Ordainer, breathed a new life into every human frame, and instilled into every word a fresh potency. All created things proclaim the evidences of this world-wide regeneration... He hath lent a fresh impulse, and set a new direction, to the birds of men's hearts... The whole earth is illuminated with the resplendent glory of God's Revelation... Behold how the generality of mankind hath been endued with the capacity to hearken unto God's most exalted Word—the Word upon which must depend the gathering together and spiritual resurrection of all men... (*Gleanings* 92–7).

'Abdu'l-Bahá adds His voice to that of His Father: "In every Dispensation, the light of Divine Guidance has been focussed upon one central theme... In this wondrous Revelation... the foundation of the Faith of God and the distinguishing feature of His Law is the consciousness of the Oneness of Mankind" (*World Order* 36).

In the original texts, a word which appears quite often to denote the newness and uniqueness of the Faith and its wondrous message is "Badí'". For example, the title given to the new Bahá'í calendar is the "Badí'" calendar. Also, Bahá'u'lláh bestowed the title "Badí'" on the 17-year-old youth who was the bearer of His Tablet to the Sháh of Persia. And, referring to "Badí'", He wrote in one of His Tablets, as if to expound the meaning of this title, "the spirit of might and power was breathed" in him (*God Passes By* 199). This word has been translated into English by Shoghi Effendi in various ways, depending on the context. The equivalents he has given are "new", "wondrous", "wonderful", "marvellous", "incomparable", and "peerless". For example, the "new World Order" in the original is God's "Badí'" World Order.

It would be helpful to cast a quick glance at the titles found in former scriptures which define the station of Bahá'u'lláh and the uniqueness of His Day. For example, Isaiah refers to Him as "the Wonderful" and "the Prince of Peace" (*God Passes By* 94). Haggai refers to Him as the "Desire for all nations" (95). Ezekiel extols Him as "the Lord Who shall be king over all the earth".

Zoroaster prophesies that the Promised One will "usher in an era of blessedness and peace".

Jesus Christ, in the Lord's Prayer, prays for the Father's "Kingdom" to come and refers to His Day as a period of "regeneration" (96). Christ's chief Apostle, Peter, refers to His Day as "the times of refreshing" and "the times of restitution of all things". St John the Divine refers to His Revelation and His Law as "a new heaven and a new earth".

Muḥammad describes His Day as a time "when the earth shall shine with the light of her Lord".

Bahá'u'lláh Himself, referring to His Day, calls it the "Springtime which autumn will never overtake" (99), the "Day which shall never be followed by night", and "the eye to past ages and centuries". He bestows on the city of Ṭihrán, where He was born, the surname of "the Mother of the world" (102), as well as the "the Source of the joy of all mankind".

He further proclaims, "I testify before God to the greatness, the inconceivable greatness of this Revelation. Again and again have We in most of Our Tablets borne witness to this truth, that mankind may be roused from its heedlessness" (*World Order* 103). "The Hand of Omnipotence hath established His Revelation upon an unassailable, an enduring foundation. Storms of human strife are powerless to undermine its basis, nor will men's fanciful theories succeed in damaging its structure" (109). "The day is approaching when God will have, by an act of His Will, raised up a race of men the nature of which is inscrutable to all save God, the All-Powerful, the Self-Subsisting" (109–10).

The Words of 'Abdu'l-Bahá are equally emphatic on this important theme. He writes, "The effulgence of God's splendorous mercy hath enveloped the peoples and kindreds of the earth, and the whole world is bathed in its shining glory..." (*World Order* 111). "Centuries, nay ages, must pass away ere the Day-Star of Truth shineth again in its mid-summer splendour or appeareth once more in the radiance of its vernal glory... How thankful must we be for having been made in this Day the recipients of so overwhelming a favour!" (111). "Whatsoever is latent in the innermost of this holy cycle shall gradually appear and be made manifest, for now is but the beginning of its growth and the dayspring of the revelation of its signs" (146).

Shoghi Effendi extols Bahá'u'lláh in such titles as "the Fountain of the Most Great Justice", the "Proclaimer of the coming of age of the entire human race", and the "Organizer of the entire planet" (*God Passes By* 93).

Against this panoramic view of the vastness, greatness, and uniqueness of the Dispensation inaugurated by Bahá'u'lláh, we should look with our finite minds at the wondrous Order which He has bequeathed to mankind. We must recall that the Covenant of Bahá'u'lláh is mentioned in the very first sentence of His Kitáb-i-'Ahd. Shoghi Effendi has identified the "excellent and priceless Heritage" in that sentence as being Bahá'u'lláh's Covenant, bequeathed by Him to His "heirs" (*God Passes By* 314). It is important to realize that we are Bahá'u'lláh's "heirs" and that the "heritage" He hath bequeathed to us is His Covenant.

The Administrative Order is the child of that Covenant, the fruition of God's Covenant for this Day. The Bahá'í Covenant is unique, and 'Abdu'l-Bahá tells us that it is "one of the distinctive features of this most mighty cycle", a Covenant "the like of which the sacred Dispensations of the past have never witnessed" (*God Passes By* 239).

Proclaiming the wondrous and unique character of this Order, Bahá'u'lláh has written in the Kitáb-i-Aqdas, "The world's equilibrium hath been upset through the vibrating influence of this most great, this new World Order. Mankind's ordered life hath been revolutionized through the agency of this unique, this wondrous system—the like of which mortal eyes have never witnessed" (¶181).

Of all the living religions in the world, Christianity and Islám are the two whose followers cherish in their hearts the aspiration of conquering the hearts of all men and of promoting their Faith to make it the dominant religion throughout the world. They have an elaborate system of missionary work in most countries of the third world. This activity involves, for example, construction of schools and hospitals open only to those who are ready to convert, grants of free scholarships for advanced studies abroad, distribution of free literature, and the erection of prayer houses, such as churches and mosques.

In recent decades, Buddhism has succeeded in winning converts, particularly in the West; but far from being used to aggressively pursue activities aimed at a world-unifying system of Buddhism, it remains merely a gentle philosophy, primarily concerned with mental and moral self-purification. It appears to me that it is because of the above observation that Shoghi Effendi confines himself to comparing the Bahá'í system of world solidarity only to the religious organizations we find in Christianity and Islám.

In comparing the Administrative Order of the Faith to systems of administration established by Christianity and Islám, Shoghi Effendi, in his letter of March 1930 to the friends throughout the West, invites them to consider the following questions:

Where and how does this Order established by Bahá'u'lláh, which to outward seeming is but a replica of the institutions established in Christianity and Islám, differ from them? Are not the twin institutions of the House of Justice and of the Guardianship, the institution of the Hands of the Cause of God, the institution of the national and local Assemblies, the institution of the Mashriqu'l-Adhkár, but different names for the institutions of the Papacy and the Caliphate, with all their attending ecclesiastical orders which the Christians and Moslems uphold and advocate? What can possibly be the agency that can safeguard these Bahá'í institutions, so strikingly resemblant, in some of their features, to those which have been reared by the Fathers of the Church and the Apostles of Muḥammad, from witnessing the deterioration in character, the breach of unity, and the extinction of influence, which have befallen all organized religious hierarchies? Why should they not eventually suffer the self-same fate that has overtaken the institutions which the successors of Christ and Muḥammad have reared? (*World Order* 18–19)

Turning his incisive mind on the weaknesses of the Christian Dispensation, Shoghi Effendi wrote the following:

None, I feel, will question the fact that the fundamental reason why the unity of the Church of Christ was irretrievably shattered, and its influence was in the course of time undermined, was that the Edifice which the Fathers of the Church reared after the passing of His First Apostle was an Edifice that rested in nowise upon the explicit directions of Christ Himself. The authority and features of their administration were wholly inferred, and indirectly derived, with more or less justification, from certain vague and fragmentary references which they found scattered amongst His utterances as recorded in the Gospel. Not one of the sacraments of the Church; not one of the rites and ceremonies which the Christian Fathers have elaborately devised and ostentatiously observed; not one of the elements of the severe discipline they rigorously imposed upon the primitive Christians; none of these reposed on the direct authority of Christ, or emanated from His specific utterances. Not one of these did Christ conceive, none did He specifically invest with sufficient authority to either interpret His Word, or to add to what He had not specifically enjoined. (*World Order* 20)

Commenting on the inherent faults in the administration of the Muḥammadan Dispensation, Shoghi Effendi wrote the following:

In the Muḥammadan Revelation… although His Faith as compared with that of Christ was, so far as the administration of His Dispensation is concerned, more complete and more specific in its provisions, yet in the matter of succession, it gave no written, no binding and conclusive instructions to those whose mission was to propagate His Cause. For the text of the Qur'án, the ordinances of which regarding prayer, fasting, marriage, divorce, inheritance, pilgrimage, and the like, have after the revolution of thirteen hundred years remained intact and operative, gives no definite guidance regarding the Law of Succession, the source of all the dissensions, the controversies, and schisms which have dismembered and discredited Islám. (*World Order* 21)

Summarizing his thoughts on the subject, the Guardian wrote the following:

The Administrative Order... it should be noted, is, by virtue of its origin and character, unique in the annals of the world's religious systems. No Prophet before Bahá'u'lláh, it can be confidently asserted... has established, authoritatively and in writing, anything comparable to the Administrative Order which the authorized Interpreter of Bahá'u'lláh's teachings has instituted, an Order which, by virtue of the administrative principles which its Author has formulated, the institutions He has established, and the right of interpretation with which He has invested its Guardian, must and will, in a manner unparalleled in any previous religion, safeguard from schism the Faith from which it has sprung. (*God Passes By* 326)

These words of Shoghi Effendi are weapons and tools with which we can proclaim the Cause and defend its interests. He further states:

...unlike all the Dispensations of the past, the apostles of Bahá'u'lláh in every land, wherever they labor and toil, have before them in clear, in unequivocal and emphatic language, all the laws, the regulations, the principles, the institutions, the guidance, they require for the prosecution and consummation of their task. Both in the administrative provisions of the Bahá'í Dispensation, and in the matter of succession, as embodied in the twin institutions of the House of Justice and of the Guardianship, the followers of Bahá'u'lláh can summon to their aid such irrefutable evidences of Divine Guidance that none can resist, that none can belittle or ignore. Therein lies the distinguishing feature of the Bahá'í Revelation. Therein lies the strength of the unity of the Faith, of the validity of a Revelation that claims not to destroy or belittle previous Revelations, but to connect, unify, and fulfil them. (*World Order* 21–2)

The Báb expounded a fundamental truth in His Persian Bayán when He wrote, "The path to guidance is one of love and compassion, not of force and coercion. This hath been God's method in the past, and shall continue to be in the future!" (*Selections from the Writings of the Báb* 77).

Unfortunately, in the history of past religions, we have seen all forms of coercion used by religious leaders and by rulers who were influenced by them. The main reason is that no specific Covenant, no authoritative central authority existed to keep the faithful on the straight path.

Another result of the absence of a documented Covenant in previous Dispensations was that religious leaders resorted to producing and promoting individual interpretations. Quite often, such interpretations were contradictory and led to sectarianism, religious conflict, and even warfare within the ranks of its own religion.

The distinctive feature of Bahá'u'lláh's Revelation is His "heritage" to us, "His heirs", that is, His Covenant. 'Abdu'l-Bahá, the Mystery of God, is its Centre, and from it have issued forth two subordinate agencies, the Guardianship and the Universal House of Justice. These two entities, while orbiting and revolving around the Centre of the Covenant, receive their inspiration directly from Bahá'u'lláh and the Báb, as clearly stipulated in the Master's Will and Testament.

We can conclude perhaps by saying that God's "Revelation" (vaḥy) is like heaven and is represented by the appearance of the Twin Manifestations, or Suns, of this Dispensation, the central one being Bahá'u'lláh. Every heaven has an earth. The earth of God's Revelation is His world of "creation", or the community of its supporters and followers.

Between the two worlds of "Revelation" and "Creation" is the world of "Inspiration" (Ilhám). In this Dispensation, "Inspiration" is represented first and foremost by 'Abdu'l-Bahá, the "Moon" of God's Holy Dispensation and the Being "round Whom all names revolve" (*World Order* 134).

The satellites that revolve round the "Moon" are the Guardianship and the Universal House of Justice. These two entities, while orbiting the Moon, receive their inspiration, as I noted, directly from Bahá'u'lláh and the Báb, as attested by the Master's Will and Testament. We could, in the end, give ourselves the courage to infer from the above that the intermediate world of "inspiration", which is between heaven and earth, is the world of "what lieth between them", repeatedly referred to in the Writings of the Báb.

We should turn our thoughts now to secular forms of government currently established in the world, showing the similarities and dissimilarities which exist between them and the Bahá'í Administrative Order. Fortunately, Shoghi Effendi has written extensively on this subject. He refers in his "Dispensation" to the three standard types of government identified by Aristotle, namely, democracy, aristocracy, and autocracy. He then goes on to show where wholesome elements of these forms of government have been preserved and where their inherent defects have been eliminated.

He writes,

This new-born Administrative Order incorporates within its structure certain elements which are to be found in each of the three recognized forms of secular government, without being in any sense a mere replica of any one of them, and without introducing within its machinery any of the objectionable features which they inherently possess. It blends and harmonizes, as no government fashioned by mortal hands has as yet accomplished, the salutary truths which each of these systems undoubtedly contains without vitiating the integrity of those God-given verities on which it is ultimately founded. (*World Order* 152–3)

Shoghi Effendi, commenting on the unique character of the Administrative Order, has given us this further insight:

Neither in theory nor in practice can the Administrative Order of the Faith of Bahá'u'lláh be said to conform to any type of democratic government, to any system of autocracy, [or] to any purely aristocratic order... The hereditary authority which the Guardian of the Administrative Order is called upon to exercise, and the right of the interpretation of the Holy Writ solely conferred upon him; the powers and prerogatives of the Universal House of Justice, possessing the exclusive right to legislate on matters not explicitly revealed in the Most Holy Book; the ordinance exempting its members from any responsibility to those whom they represent, and from the obligation to conform to their views, convictions or sentiments; the specific provisions requiring the free and democratic election by the mass of the faithful of the Body that constitutes the sole legislative organ in the world-wide Bahá'í community—these are among the features which combine to set apart the Order identified with the Revelation of Bahá'u'lláh from any of the existing systems of human government. (*God Passes By* 326–7)

It would be useful to consider the definitions of the terms to describe the three standard forms of secular government as identified by Aristotle. "Democracy" is government by the people, of the people, and for the people. "Aristocracy" is government by a select few, who, by virtue of their exceptionally high privileges, act independently of the views and opinions of the people. "Autocracy" is government by one person or one agency, whose judgement is not subject to the authority or control of others. Thus, the locus of authority of the three forms of government ranges from all people, to a select few, to one entity.

What remain to be identified are these features of the three forms of secular government that are regarded as wholesome in character and which are found in the Administrative Order and those aspects that are considered deficient and therefore not incorporated in the Bahá'í system.

I recall discussions on this subject during the ministry of Shoghi Effendi and the manner in which students and scholars of the Faith identified these features. "Autocracy", in its divinely ordained form, was seen in the institution of the Guardianship. "Aristocracy" was identified with the institution of the Hands of the Cause of God. "Democracy" was associated with the elected members of the Universal House of Justice.

However, after the passing of Shoghi Effendi and the realization that the Guardianship was no longer with us as a continuing institution, and furthermore, when the House of Justice decided that it could not appoint or make it possible to appoint Hands of the Cause of God, it was clear that these elements of the Administrative Order, as they existed during the ministry of Shoghi Effendi, could not be replicated after his passing.

In other words, just as the rudiments of the Administrative Order as they existed during the ministry of 'Abdu'l-Bahá were temporary, likewise, the scheme of Bahá'í Administration as it was operative during the ministry of Shoghi Effendi could not be duplicated.

This point appeared in even sharper relief when it was noted in Shoghi Effendi's "Dispensation" that before introducing his theme on the differences between the Administrative Order and the three forms of secular government, he clearly states that his intention is to clarify the "theory" on which the Administrative Order is based (*World Order* 152). Therefore, we all had to look at the basic principles governing the existing chief institutions of the Administrative Order, in anticipation of the time when they will become the nucleus and pattern of the World Order of Bahá'u'lláh.

For example, Shoghi Effendi clearly points out in the "Dispensation" that the basis on which the Bahá'í Administrative Order has been structured makes it inclined "to democratic methods in the administration of its affairs" (*World Order* 154). However, when one reads the Will and Testament of 'Abdu'l-Bahá on the subject of the range of authority of the Guardian of the Faith, one can easily notice that he was invested with unchallengeable powers in relation to the Hands of the Cause, whom he could appoint and dismiss at his own discretion, as well as the elected members of the House of Justice, who are required "to show their obedience, submissiveness and subordination unto the Guardian of the Cause of God, to turn unto him and be lowly before him" (*Will and Testament* 11). According to the Will and Testament, all the friends are included in this act of obedience; and indeed, as the Will stipulates, "all the Aghṣán, the Afnán [and] the Hands of the Cause of God" should abide by the decisions and guidance of the Guardian of the Cause (11). The Guardian was further empowered, according to the terms of the Will, to expel any member of the House of Justice who, in his estimation, had committed "a sin, injurious to the common weal" (14). Surely such a scenario characterizes the Bahá'í Administrative Order as a System heavily inclined not towards democratic practices but towards autocratic methods in the administration of the Cause.

We should also recall that in his "Dispensation" Shoghi Effendi states that while 'Abdu'l-Bahá does not possess the station of Prophethood, He was endowed with "superhuman knowledge and perfection" (*World Order* 134). In the light of this statement, and faced as we are with the physical absence of a Guardian in the Administrative Order, could we not venture to assume that 'Abdu'l-Bahá had indeed envisaged two stages in the development of the Administrative Order after Him: one, a temporary stage, with the Guardian at its Head and with the element of autocracy as its dominant characteristic, and the other to be extended into the future, with the Universal House of

Justice as its Supreme Organ and with the element of democracy as its dominant characteristic?

Let us now contrast the Administrative Order with secular governments. For example, the election of the members of the Universal House of Justice and of the members of Spiritual Assemblies, both national and local, (although free of nomination and campaigning) is purely democratic in character. Likewise, the method of Bahá'í consultation (although far superior in dignity and harmony to what we see in parliamentary debates in the legislative councils of the world) is yet another democratic feature incorporated in the Bahá'í administrative system. A third democratic feature is the degree of autonomy provided to elected councils on the national and local levels. This is an element of decentralization in administrative affairs which is increasingly being applied and appreciated in many democratic countries of the world. The obvious dissimilarity is that under the Bahá'í system, the elected are not responsible to those who elect them. A moral and spiritual responsibility is attached to the work of elected members, and, therefore, their conscientious responsibility is to God and to God alone, as ordained and stressed in the teachings of our Faith.

As to aristocracy, a trace of similarity is the existence of the institution of the Counsellors on the international and continental levels as well as the Auxiliary Board members and their assistants for circumscribed geographical areas. However, these appointed individuals do not possess decision-making authority, and their function, in the final analysis, is purely advisory in nature, unlike an aristocratic system, which invests small and select groups with special powers and privileges. A clear similarity is in the fact that decision-making authority in the Administrative Order lies with the elected few—namely, members of Local and National Assemblies and members of the Supreme Body—all of whom are not responsible to their respective electorates. However, its dissimilarity is that the elected members of these councils are not a class of nobility, nor do they assume their positions on the basis of birth or inheritance. In the Administrative Order, they are in their position of authority because of the democratic procedure of Bahá'í elections.

Finally, as to autocracy, the similarity, as the Constitution of the Universal House of Justice clearly stipulates, is that

> The provenance, the authority, the duties, the sphere of action of the Universal House of Justice all derive from the revealed Word of Bahá'u'lláh which, together with the interpretations and expositions of the Centre of the Covenant and of the Guardian of the Cause—who, after 'Abdu'l-Bahá, is the sole authority in the interpretation of Bahá'í Scripture—constitute the binding terms of reference of the Universal House of Justice and are its bedrock foundation. The authority of these Texts is absolute and immutable until such time as Almighty God shall reveal His new Manifestation to Whom will belong all authority and power. (*Constitution* 4)

Thus, the autocratic character of the Administrative Order is the divine authority vested in the Holy Writ of the Author of the Faith and the two authorized interpreters of His revealed Word. The dissimilarity lies in the fact that there is an unlimited field of legislation in subsidiary matters in which to supplement the laws revealed by Bahá'u'lláh, to apply these laws and ordinances universally, and to legislate on matters not explicitly covered by the Sacred Text and its authoritative interpretation. These responsibilities are discharged by the Universal House of Justice, which is the Supreme Legislature of the Bahá'í World Commonwealth.

I would like to end this section with the categorical assurance given by the Guardian of our Faith, looking into the future, as the Administrative Order of Bahá'u'lláh expands and develops to meet the challenges of an ever-evolving, ever-advancing civilization. Shoghi Effendi writes,

The admitted evils inherent in each of these systems being rigidly and permanently excluded, this unique Order, however long it may endure and however extensive its ramifications, cannot ever degenerate into any form of despotism, of oligarchy, or of demagogy which must sooner or later corrupt the machinery of all man-made and essentially defective political institutions. (*World Order* 154)

The three words "despotism", "oligarchy", and "demagogy" need some clarification. Despotism means dictatorship or aggressive governance by a tyrant ruler. Oligarchy means control of a government by a small clique of selfish and corrupt rulers. Demagogy means government by self-seeking elected political leaders who make false promises to the electorate and feed on the prejudices and ignorance of the people.

Shoghi Effendi, the inspired interpreter of our teachings, is giving us the assurance that none of the evils of these harmful forms of government will ever assail and corrupt the divinely ordained and divinely propelled Administrative Order, arrest its maturation into the World Order, or impede its final fruition into the Bahá'í Commonwealth of the future.

There is a wonderful letter from the beloved Guardian, written in Persian in 1929, to the Bahá'ís of Iran. Some heartbreaking persecutions had taken place in the Cradle of the Faith, and, in this letter, Shoghi Effendi calls on the Persian friends to be patient and to continue to cling to the hem of the robe of God's Holy Faith. God is watchful, and His invisible hand is at work. At the appointed time, fair-minded academics, although they will not be Bahá'ís, will arise to defend the Cause and claim for the believers their legitimate rights.

Shoghi Effendi has taught us how to present the Faith and the distinctive features of its World Order to the outside world. Bahá'í youth, as serious students and scholars of the Faith, should be able to explain to open-minded professors and earnestly seeking fellow students in a wise way the excellence and perfection of the Bahá'í system of World Order, without ever giving the impression that they are seeking to win over such individuals to the Faith. For it will be from among such erudite, impartial, and unbiased academics and intellectuals that courageous leaders of thought will arise and be moved to objectively and fairly defend the Faith and vindicate its right to exist in Iran as well as in the countries where its followers are persecuted.

The world is now passing through a period of godlessness. It will not be long before it gradually turns its back to materialism and acknowledges its need for religion. Of course, as Bahá'ís, we have a major role to play in bringing about this awareness—an awareness which will surely and eventually lead to the spiritualization of the masses and, ultimately, to a wholehearted acceptance of the validity and reality of the Faith of the Blessed Beauty. What I am outlining is based on my understanding of the teachings on this subject.

As Bahá'í youth, we should prepare ourselves for these exciting developments and beg Bahá'u'lláh to accept us and use us as instruments for the realization of His purpose. If we feel unworthy, it does not matter. In fact, that is how it must be. Let us place our trust in Him and face the future with confidence and optimism.

Questions related:

Q. As Bahá'ís, we are asked to collaborate with associations and governments that are in harmony with the Bahá'í vision. How can we do this without being associated with political parties and being corrupted by their policies?

A. Our teachings clearly indicate that we should associate with all strata of society, and this includes religious leaders, political figures, leaders of thought, and the rank and file of society. If we have any doubt about political parties, we should consult our National Spiritual Assembly.

The important thing is to have the courage and determination to mix with people at all levels. God will show us those who are receptive. He will either send them to us or guide us to them.

Q. What is the meaning of "a springtime which autumn will never overtake" and "a day which will never be followed by night"?

A. As I understand it, these concepts refer to the Covenant. Bahá'u'lláh is giving us the assurance that His Faith will not be subjected to sectarianism and divisions within the community, as has occurred in other systems. It will remain united throughout the Dispensation. Indeed, 'Abdu'l-Bahá has gone so far as to state that "the power of the Covenant is the pivot of the oneness of mankind" (*God Passes By* 238).

Q. In the fifth Glad Tidings, Bahá'u'lláh refers to a republican form of government which profits the people, but at the same time He praises the majesty of kingship. He finally says that the two forms should be combined into one. What does this mean?

A. In the Tablet of the World, Bahá'u'lláh says, "The system of government which the British people have adopted in London appeareth to be good, for it is adorned with the light of both kingship and of the consultation of the people" (*Tablets of Bahá'u'lláh* 93). I think Bahá'u'lláh is referring to constitutional monarchy as being an acceptable national system of government.

Q. How can we explain to non-Bahá'ís the role and function of our Supreme Body?

A. I suggest we avoid using the term "infallibility" too loosely when we are introducing the Faith to enquirers. We should refer to the Universal House of Justice as the supreme elected council of the Bahá'í community, it being also the Head of the Faith.

When discussing the role of the West or of America in helping to shape the fortunes of the Faith, it is important to make distinctions based on exact geographical terms used in the Writings. For example, at times it is simply "the West". At other times it is "the Americas", that is, the continent of America or the western hemisphere. There is also reference to "North America", implying the United States and Canada. And finally, the word "America" is used on its own quite often to mean the United States of America.

At the very outset of His mission, the Báb revealed His first book, the Qayyúmu'l-Asmá; and in it He addresses "the peoples of the West" and calls on them to "issue forth" from their "cities" to aid God and to "become as brethren" in His "one and indivisible religion" (*God Passes By* 253).

As far as we can determine, the first reference from the Pen of Bahá'u'lláh to the role that is to be played by the republics of the western hemisphere appears in the Kitáb-i-Aqdas when He addresses the "Rulers of America and the Presidents of the Republics therein". This passage in the Kitáb-i-Aqdas consists of one whole paragraph and has seven sentences. The entire passage is as follows:

> Hearken ye, O Rulers of America and the Presidents of the Republics therein, unto that which the Dove is warbling on the Branch of Eternity: "There is none other God but Me, the Ever-Abiding, the Forgiving, the All-Bountiful." Adorn ye the temple of dominion with the ornament of justice and of the fear of God, and its head with the crown of the remembrance of your Lord, the Creator of the heavens. Thus counselleth you He Who is the Dayspring of Names, as bidden by Him Who is the All-Knowing, the All-Wise.

The Promised One hath appeared in this glorified Station, whereat all beings, both seen and unseen, have rejoiced. Take ye advantage of the Day of God. Verily, to meet Him is better for you than all that whereon the sun shineth, could ye but know it. O concourse of rulers! Give ear unto that which hath been raised from the Dayspring of Grandeur: "Verily, there is none other God but Me, the Lord of Utterance, the All-Knowing." Bind ye the broken with the hands of justice, and crush the oppressor who flourisheth with the rod of the commandments of your Lord, the Ordainer, the All-Wise. (¶88)

The first five sentences, which end with the words "could ye but know it", deal with justice, the fear of God, the need to remember Him, and the appearance of the Promised One. When I was in Persia and attended classes on the Aqdas conducted by scholars of the Faith, the explanation given to us of this passage was that the first five sentences were addressed to the rulers of the American continent, but that the last two sentences, introduced by the words "O concourse of rulers", referred to all rulers throughout the planet.

It was in June 1947 that Shoghi Effendi, in a letter addressed to the American Bahá'í community, gave for the first time his translation of this section of the Kitáb-i-Aqdas. It was then that we realized that Shoghi Effendi's understanding was different from that of our scholars, as his translation made the "rulers of America" and the "concourse of rulers" one and the same group of leaders.

I repeat that the importance of this translation of the Guardian is in his interpretation that the instruction incorporated in the last two sentences is not an assignment to all rulers throughout the planet but is an expression of God's Will giving a mission specifically to the rulers throughout the western hemisphere. I will repeat the last two sentences to show how important they are, not only from a Bahá'í point of view but also in terms of the political situation on the world scene:

> O concourse of rulers! Give ear unto that which hath been raised from the Dayspring of Grandeur: "Verily, there is none other God but Me, the Lord of Utterance, the All-Knowing." Bind ye the broken with the hands of justice, and crush the oppressor who flourisheth with the rod of the commandments of your Lord, the Ordainer, the All-Wise. (¶88).

As you see, the rulers of the western hemisphere are commissioned by Bahá'u'lláh to "bind the broken" and "crush the oppressor". "The broken", in my view, is primarily a reference to the broken bones of Bahá'í communities living under oppressive and tyrannical regimes in the East, and more particularly in Iran. This word, of course, also refers in a general way to all downtrodden and persecuted minority groups throughout the world.

The mission given by Bahá'u'lláh does not end there, as the rulers of the Americas are further commissioned to "crush the oppressor who flourisheth". This calls to mind a Hidden Word of Bahá'u'lláh: "O OPPRESSORS ON EARTH! Withdraw your hands from tyranny, for I have pledged Myself not to forgive any man's injustice. This is My covenant which I have irrevocably decreed in the preserved tablet and sealed with My seal" (Hidden Words, Persian, no. 64). While in the first instance, this is a specific obligation that Bahá'u'lláh has placed directly on the shoulders of the rulers holding the reins of power and authority in the western hemisphere, this does not mean that rulers in other parts of the world can ignore acts of injustice. It merely indicates that the rulers in the western hemisphere are expected by the Almighty to be at the forefront of those who succour the oppressed, stay the hand of the oppressors, and inflict punishment on them.

It is interesting that the tone of Bahá'u'lláh's address to the rulers of the American continent, although one of authority and command, is different from the tone of His Tablets to the other rulers or kings of the world. In these Tablets one notes expressions of rebuke and censure and at times even of warnings of divine chastisement.

Another momentous utterance of Bahá'u'lláh is His Prophecy about the sovereignty which His Revelation will achieve through those who will champion His Faith in the West. He says, "In the East the light of His Revelation hath broken; in the West have appeared the signs of His dominion. Ponder this in your hearts, O people, and be not of those who have turned a deaf ear to the admonitions of Him Who is the Almighty, the All-Praised" (*World Order* 78).

Bahá'u'lláh is also reported to have said, "Had this Cause been revealed in the West... it would have become evident how the people of the Occident would have embraced our Cause" (*God Passes By* 253).

Commenting on the same theme, 'Abdu'l-Bahá has written,

From the beginning of time until the present day... the light of Divine Revelation hath risen in the East and shed its radiance upon the West. The illumination thus shed hath, however, acquired in the West an extraordinary brilliancy. Consider the Faith proclaimed by Jesus. Though it first appeared in the East, yet not until its light had been shed upon the West did the full measure of its potentialities become manifest. The day is approaching... when ye shall witness how, through the splendor of the Faith of Bahá'u'lláh, the West will have replaced the East, radiating the light of Divine guidance. (*God Passes By* 253–4)

Elaborating on this same subject, Shoghi Effendi describes Europe as "the scene of the greatest exploits of the followers of Jesus Christ" and, likewise, where "some of the most resplendent victories which ushered in the Golden Age of Islám" were won (*Citadel of Faith* 27).

It should be pointed out here that Christianity and Islám certainly had covenants; but, as we saw in Shoghi Effendi's comments, these covenants were not as firm and unchallengeable as the one we find in the Cause of Bahá'u'lláh. It is worth noting, therefore, that St Paul, who had strained and unpleasant relations with St Peter, the rightful Successor, was able to play a major role in the spread of the Faith of Christ on European soil. Likewise, in Islám, it was the Sunní branch of that Faith—not the Shí'ih sect, which clung to the legitimate Law of Succession— that was able to usher in the Golden Age of Islám on the European continent. Thus we see that, with covenants in former dispensations being vague and fluid, God seems to have permitted those who had disavowed their provisions and even flouted them—like St Paul in Christianity and the Sunní leaders in Islám—to lead the way for a prescribed period to exploits and victories under the banner of God's Holy Cause.

We must recall that the West was not opened to the light of the Faith during the Ministry of Bahá'u'lláh. One year after His Ascension in September 1893 we see a landmark in the history of the Faith in the western hemisphere when, for the first time, the Faith was publicly mentioned at the World Parliament of Religions in Chicago. Soon after this event, the first wave of new believers came under the shadow of the Cause of God; and in December 1898 the first group of American pilgrims visited the Shrine of Bahá'u'lláh and were received as guests in the Home of 'Abdu'l-Bahá. No doubt one of the principal objectives of the Master's ministry was to visit North America to encourage and deepen the followers of His Father's Faith and to lay the cornerstone of a House of Worship, which became the Mother Temple of the West.

During the course of the First World War, between 1916 and 1917, and under the influence of and inspired by the address of Bahá'u'lláh to the rulers of the Americas, as attested by Shoghi

Effendi, 'Abdu'l-Bahá revealed the Tablets of the Divine Plan, addressed to the two Bahá'í communities of the United States and Canada. Shoghi Effendi identified these Tablets as the charter for the promulgation of the Faith throughout the world *(Messages to the Bahá'í World* 84). These Tablets invest the American Bahá'í community with what Shoghi Effendi referred to as a unique spiritual primacy (*World Order* 77).

The Words of 'Abdu'l-Bahá about the American Bahá'í community and its future achievements are indeed most impressive:

> Behold the portals which Bahá'u'lláh hath opened before you! Consider how exalted and lofty is the station you are destined to attain; how unique the favors with which you have been endowed... The full measure of your success... is as yet unrevealed, its significance still unapprehended... The range of your future achievements... still remains undisclosed... The moment this Divine Message is carried forward by the American believers from the shores of America and is propagated through the continents of Europe, of Asia, of Africa and of Australasia, and as far as the islands of the Pacific, this community will find itself securely established upon the throne of an everlasting dominion. Then will all the peoples of the world witness that this community is spiritually illumined and divinely guided. Then will the whole earth resound with the praises of its majesty and greatness. (*World Order* 77–8)

Such is its glorious destiny.

During the latter period of the ministry of 'Abdu'l-Bahá, He could see the first fruits of the exploits achieved by the American Bahá'í community, such accomplishments as the establishment of Chicago's first House of Spirituality, the formation of the Bahá'í Publishing Society, the founding of the Green Acre Fellowship, the publication of *The Star of the West*, the incorporation of the Bahá'í Temple Unity subsequent to the holding of the first National Bahá'í Convention, and the formation of the Executive Committee of the Mashriqu'l-Adhkár. These developments were all achievements in the administrative field of Bahá'í service. On the teaching front, 'Abdu'l-Bahá was able to witness members of the American Bahá'í community serve as pioneers or travelling teachers to Alaska, as well as to Europe, France, Great Britain, and Germany, and in addition to the Baltic States, the Balkan Peninsula, and Scandinavia. And He rejoiced as the teaching work extended beyond the European continent to the West Indies, Latin America, South Africa, China, Japan, India, Tahiti, the Australian continent, and as far as Tasmania and New Zealand. When 'Abdu'l-Bahá passed away, the light of the Faith of His Father had already reached 35 countries of the world. These countries were opened partly by friends from the East but were opened for the most part by believers from the United States.

With the inception of the Formative Age of the Faith after the passing of 'Abdu'l-Bahá, Shoghi Effendi had to lay down the foundations of the Administrative Order along the broad lines outlined in 'Abdu'l-Bahá's Will and Testament. He called on Bahá'í communities in the East and West to establish their Local Spiritual Assemblies on a sound basis and to establish National Spiritual Assemblies as soon as it was propitious to do so.

Shoghi Effendi focused his special attention on the Bahá'í communities of the United States and Canada, which at that time constituted one single home front, giving them specific and essential instructions on administrative principles governing the work of the Faith. After calling the American believers "the spiritual descendants of the Dawn–Breakers", he praised their dedication to the Cause and encouraged them to follow in the footsteps of the heroes of an earlier age by becoming self-sacrificing living martyrs. It was not long after that he called the

American Bahá'í community "the Cradle of the Administrative Order".

Soon after, Shoghi Effendi explained that God had chosen that country to be thus distinguished by reason of the patent evils that were rampant in the lives of its people. The evils he enumerated, and which would stand in contrast to the virtues and perfections of the builders of God's Administrative Order, are as follows: (1) immersion "in a sea of materialism", (2) "a prey to one of the most virulent and long-standing forms of racial prejudice", and (3) a victim of "political corruption, lawlessness and laxity in moral standards" (*Advent* 19).

Before the United States became the Cradle of the Administrative Order, Persia had been designated the Cradle of the Faith itself. For the same purpose of contrasting evil with virtue, Shoghi Effendi, looking at Persia of the nineteenth century, describes the Cradle of the Faith as "the most backward, the most cowardly, and perverse of peoples"—a nation that had "sunk to such ignominious depths, and manifested so great a perversity, as to find no parallel among its contemporaries" (*Advent* 10). From out of such a population, the Revelation of Bahá'u'lláh was able to raise up heroes, martyrs, and saints who will always be the pride and glory of this Dispensation.

For over 16 years, Shoghi Effendi did not cease to give general and detailed guidance to the American National Spiritual Assembly to enable it to erect a perfect structure, as called for in 'Abdu'l-Bahá's Will and Testament. This document, as we saw in a previous section, was named by Shoghi Effendi as the Charter of the future world civilization. The document was already known by the more modest title of "Charter for the Establishment of the Administrative Order", since the Administrative Order would lead to the World Order, which in turn would ultimately give birth to the world Bahá'í civilization.

These 16 years were difficult years for Shoghi Effendi. Covenant-breakers in the West, like Ahmad Sohrab, attacked him for concentrating on administrative matters and accused him of ignoring the provisions of the Tablets of the Divine Plan. They could not see nor appreciate what Shoghi Effendi was doing. He was patiently building up the Administrative Order and its institutions in order to use them as instruments for the systematic implementation of the Master's vision. He had to explain to the friends that the Administrative Order was not an innovation being imposed on the Bahá'ís of the world, but that, as soon as it acquired a reasonable degree of efficiency, its agencies would be used to advance the primary purpose for which they were intended and ordained in the Writings.

After these 16 years, Shoghi Effendi told the American believers that they were now ready to launch the first stage of the implementation of the other charter created by 'Abdu'l-Bahá and described by Shoghi Effendi as the charter for the promulgation of the Faith throughout the world, namely, the Tablets of the Divine Plan. This first stage was the first Seven Year Plan of the North American Bahá'í community. The chief objectives of this Plan, which spanned from 1937 to 1944, were (1) the completion of the exterior of the Temple in Wilmette, (2) the formation of a Spiritual Assembly in each state and province of North America and in Alaska, and (3) the establishment of a centre in each republic of Latin America and the Caribbean.

This plan was the first organized campaign of any Bahá'í community for the expansion and consolidation of the Faith in a given geographical area. It was indeed, at the same time, as I have just said, the first systematic teaching plan of the American believers, under the mandate of the Tablets of the Divine Plan.

A recent compilation entitled *This Decisive Hour* contains the messages of Shoghi Effendi to the North American Bahá'ís from 1932 to 1946. Half of the book, over 80 pages, contains messages that Shoghi Effendi sent to the North American National Spiritual Assembly during the period of its first Seven Year Plan. He guided their steps in the fulfilment of their goals, encouraging them to plod on despite their small numerical strength and the difficulties and anxieties they were encountering, praising them for their devotion, and applauding them for their dedication, loyalty, steadfastness, and the self-sacrifice they had accepted in the path of their love for the Blessed Beauty.

This first historic teaching plan of the Bahá'í world was concluded in 1944 on the eve of the 100th Anniversary of the Declaration of the Báb in Shíraz, which coincided with the opening of the second century of the Bahá'í Era. As Shoghi Effendi looked at the first 23 years of the Formative Age of the Faith, he decided that the first epoch of that Age had come to an end. The American Bahá'í community had led the Bahá'í world in laying the foundation of the Administrative Order and had used the agencies of that Order to initiate the first teaching and consolidation plan in the history of the Faith. Their victories were in the administrative as well as the teaching fields of Bahá'í service. Shoghi Effendi was pleased with them and proud of them and was offering their institutions and teaching plans as models for the entire Bahá'í world to emulate. The American believers had truly won the palm of victory.

The Bahá'í world was now ready to enter the second epoch of its Formative Age. This second epoch witnessed the launching of the second Seven Year Plan of the American Bahá'ís, which covered the period from 1946 to 1953. At the same time, Shoghi Effendi called on all other National Assemblies to launch teaching plans, depending on their special national circumstances and benefiting from the experiences of the American Bahá'í community.

It would be useful to share with you some thoughts on the subject of epochs as found in the writings of Shoghi Effendi. He visualized and projected two series, or lines, of epochs: one related to the evolution of the Formative Age, and the other to the prosecution of the provisions of the Tablets of the Divine Plan.

As to the Formative Age, its first epoch began in 1921 and ended in 1944. Shoghi Effendi later wrote that the second epoch would end in 1963, with the end of the Ten Year Plan. Under the guidance of the Universal House of Justice, two more epochs have elapsed, and we are now passing through the fifth epoch of the Formative Age.

Regarding the second line, namely, the implementation of the Tablets of the Divine Plan, Shoghi Effendi pointed out that its first epoch began in 1937, with the inception of America's first Seven Year Plan, and would end in 1963, with the termination of his Ten Year Plan. We are now in the second epoch of the Tablets of the Divine Plan, and the Universal House of Justice will determine when this second epoch will end.

Thus, Shoghi Effendi gradually prepared the entire Bahá'í world for the Great Jubilee of 1953, when he announced the 27 objectives of his world-embracing, world-shaking Ten Year Crusade. In this Ten Year Plan, Shoghi Effendi acknowledged that he had given the lion's share of its goals to the American Bahá'í community.

During his 36 years as Guardian of the Faith, he praised the American Baha'i community in innumerable messages in such terms as these:

- the envied custodians of a Divine Plan (*Citadel of Faith* 120)

- the principal builders and defenders of a mighty Order (120)

- the recognized champions of an unspeakably glorious and precious Faith (120)

- a community invested with a spiritual primacy (34)

- a richly endowed and spiritually blessed community (42)

- the executors of 'Abdu'l-Bahá's Mandate (109)

- the great-minded, stout-hearted, high-spirited American Bahá'í community (66).

- the torchbearers of a world-girdling civilization (31)

- a dearly loved, richly endowed, unflinchingly resolute community (49)

- the privileged occupants and stout-hearted defenders of the foremost citadel of the Faith (83).

- the valorous American Bahá'í Community (*Messages to the Bahá'í World* 35).

- this repeatedly blessed... community (*This Decisive Hour* ¶127.1).

- the standard-bearers of the all-conquering army of the Lord of Hosts (*Citadel of Faith* 109)

There is in the prophecies about the future contributions of the West and, more particularly, of the American believers a special emphasis on the emancipation and triumph of the Cause of God in the land of its birth. Shoghi Effendi wrote that the "promised redemption" of the Persian Bahá'í community, "as foretold by 'Abdu'l-Bahá, must first be made manifest through the efforts of their brethren" in America (*Bahá'í Administration* 117). He also quoted the following statement by the Master:

Erelong will your brethren from Europe and America journey to Persia. There they will promote to an unprecedented degree the interests of art and industry. There they will rear the institutions of true civilization, promote the development of husbandry and trade, and assist in the spread of education... Assuredly they will come; assuredly they will contribute in making of the land of Irán the envy and the admiration of the peoples and nations of the world. (173)

Looking beyond Iran, Shoghi Effendi recalled the fond hope of 'Abdu'l-Bahá that the United States would achieve universal recognition of the Faith worldwide (88).

Referring to the western hemisphere, 'Abdu'l-Bahá has written, "The continent of America... is in the eyes of the one true God the land wherein the splendors of His light shall be revealed, where the mysteries of His Faith shall be unveiled, where the righteous will abide and the free assemble" (*World Order* 75). He also wrote, "The American continent gives signs and evidences of very great advancement. Its future is even more promising, for its influence and illumination are far-reaching. It will lead all nations spiritually" (76). Note that this spiritual leadership refers not only to the United States but to the people of the entire continent.

Regarding the American nation specifically, we read the following from 'Abdu'l-Bahá: "May this American democracy... be the first nation to establish the foundation of international agreement. May it be the first nation to proclaim the unity of mankind. May it be the first to unfurl the standard of the 'Most Great Peace'" (*World Order* 75). Shoghi Effendi has drawn our attention more than once to the close resemblance of the events which led to the welding of the American states into a single federation to what is transpiring on the world scene in accordance with God's Major Plan in order to coalesce the scattered fragments into which this divided world has fallen into "one single unit, solid and indivisible, able to execute His design for the children of men" (*Promised Day Is Come* ¶203).

'Abdu'l-Bahá went so far as to advise the following to a high official serving the federal government of the United States of America who had questioned Him as to the best manner in which he could promote the interests of his government and people: "You can best serve your country... if you strive, in your capacity as a citizen of the world, to assist in the eventual application of the principle of federalism underlying the government of your own country to the relationships now existing between the peoples and nations of the world" (*World Order* 37).

This statement by 'Abdu'l-Bahá carries with it two fundamental points: (1) that the structure of federalism as conceived and practiced in the United States of America, with autonomy given to the federated States of the country, is, in 'Abdu'l-Bahá's estimation, an acceptable system of organization for the world, and (2) that the best way to promote the interests of the part is for the part to uphold the welfare of the whole.

We find this second point elaborated on more fully by Shoghi Effendi in the following statement:

...the followers of the Bahá'í Faith... viewing mankind as one entity, and profoundly attached to its vital interests, will not hesitate to subordinate every particular interest, be it personal, regional or national, to the overriding interests of the generality of mankind, knowing full well that in a world of interdependent peoples and nations the advantage of the part is best to be reached by the advantage of the whole, and that no lasting result can be achieved by any of the component parts if the general interests of the entity itself are neglected... (*Call to the Nations* xvii–xviii).

It is undoubtedly in the light of this principle of the inevitable interdependence of states and nations that Shoghi Effendi wrote the following about the destiny of America:

The world is moving on. Its events are unfolding ominously and with bewildering rapidity. The whirlwind of its passions is swift and alarmingly violent. The New World is being insensibly drawn into its vortex... The Great Republic of the West finds itself particularly and increasingly involved... The world is contracting into a neighborhood. America, willingly or unwillingly, must face and grapple with this new situation. For purposes of national security, let alone any humanitarian motive, she must assume the obligations imposed by this newly created neighborhood. Paradoxical as it may seem, her only hope of extricating herself from the perils gathering around her is to become entangled in that very web of international association which the Hand of an inscrutable Providence is weaving. (*Advent* 87–90).

Although these words of the beloved Guardian were written in December 1938, 66 years ago, they seem as if they could have been written last week. There is no doubt that they are prophetic in their essence.

To summarize, we see that Bahá'u'lláh has destined the American Bahá'í community not only to be the Cradle of the Administrative Order but also to usher in the World Order of Bahá'u'lláh and indeed the Golden Age of the Faith (*Advent* 20). In other words, it is to become the principal instrument destined to establish an entity that will grow into the Bahá'í Commonwealth of the future.

Looking into the immediate and distant future of this well-loved, divinely chosen, and highly promising community, I can do no better than to quote these words of the beloved Guardian to conclude this section:

Who knows but that [the years ahead] may not be pregnant with events of unimaginable magnitude, with ordeals more severe than any that humanity has as yet experienced, with conflicts more devastating than any which have preceded them. Dangers, however sinister, must, at no time, dim the radiance of their new-born faith. Strife and confusion, however bewildering, must never befog their vision. Tribulations, however afflictive, must never shatter their resolve. Denunciations, however clamorous, must never sap their loyalty. Upheavals, however cataclysmic, must never deflect their course... Far from yielding in their resolve, far from growing oblivious of their task, they should, at no time, however much buffeted by circumstances, forget that the synchronization of such world-shaking crises with the progressive unfoldment and fruition of their divinely appointed task is itself the work of Providence, the design of an inscrutable Wisdom, and the purpose of an all-compelling Will, a Will that directs and controls, in its own mysterious way, both the fortunes of the Faith and the destinies of men. Such simultaneous processes of rise and of fall, of integration and of disintegration, of order and chaos, with their continuous and reciprocal reactions on each other, are but aspects of a greater Plan, one and indivisible, whose Source is God, whose author is Bahá'u'lláh, the theater of whose operations is the entire planet, and whose ultimate objectives are the unity of the human race and the peace of all mankind. (*Advent* 72–3)

Shoghi Effendi gives us his vision of the destiny of America by confidently stating that the nation will

raise its voice in the councils of the nations, itself lay the cornerstone of a universal and enduring peace, proclaim the solidarity, the unity, and maturity of mankind, and assist in the establishment of the promised reign of righteousness on earth. Then, and only then, will the American nation, while the community of the American believers within its heart is consummating its divinely appointed mission, be able to fulfil the unspeakably glorious destiny ordained for it by the Almighty. (*Advent* 90–1)

Questions related:

Q. Please clarify the Guardian's description of the American community as an "envied community". The word envy has negative connotations that could be misleading.

A. The word "envy" has a double meaning in English, a negative or pejorative one and a positive one. In its negative sense it means jealousy; but in its positive sense it means an aspiration to be like another person. I believe that it is in the latter sense that we should understand the term "envied community". In Persian and Arabic we have two different words for envy: in its positive sense and in its negative sense.

Q. America's mission according to its own statement is to oust tyranny and free the oppressed. Could this not be done in a way that would validate international cooperation?

A. I do not wish to go into a commentary on the current international scene. However, in the future, Shoghi Effendi assures us that the American nation will "raise its voice in the councils of the nations" (*Advent* 90–1). To me this implies international collaboration and support.

Q. How can we assure our non-Bahá'í friends that in the future no country will maintain an army and possess armaments beyond what it needs for the safeguarding of its own territory, as is happening today?

A. The world we see today is a world in disarray, which is the result of feelings of distrust, competition, and suspicion among nations. This is likened to the stage of turbulence of the age of adolescence of the human race. Bahá'u'lláh tells us that we are at the threshold of the maturity of the world, but we have not yet entered that stage. We are looking at the world with the glasses of today, but Bahá'u'lláh could see the future. He knew the world would ripen, as a tree does. God planted this tree, and Bahá'u'lláh, the Supreme Manifestation of God for today, is looking after this tree. His view of the distant future is optimistic, not pessimistic. The immediate future, He could see, was dark, and He has said so in His Writings; but the distant future was bright, because He could see the process of an ever-evolving and ever-advancing civilization—from tribe mentality to city-state values to nationhood culture and, finally and inevitably, to a sense of world citizenship, leading to world government, world peace, and world civilization.

The Formative Age of the Faith of Bahá'u'lláh began in November 1921, with the passing of the beloved Master and the reading of His Will and Testament. For 77 years, that is, from 1844 to 1921, the Faith of Bahá'u'lláh not only was established in the land of its birth but succeeded in expanding its operation and extending the scope of its activities to 35 countries of the world.

Such a remarkable feat was realized notwithstanding the lack of an organized and systematic system to coordinate and stimulate the activities of the friends. Despite the persecution, deportation, and martyrdom of the Báb, followed by the imprisonment, repeated exiles, and close surveillance of the Author of our Faith and the Centre of His Covenant, the Cause of God survived these waves of repression thanks to the superhuman knowledge and administrative genius of the Heads of our Faith.

Through detailed instructions given by the Heads of our Faith to Letters of the Living, Apostles of Bahá'u'lláh, Disciples of 'Abdu'l-Bahá, Hands of the Cause, and other eminent teachers and promoters of the Faith, not only was the Bahá'í community protected from schism, but its ramifications continued to expand and develop. Shoghi Effendi has summarized for us in two of his letters what he describes as "the faint glimmerings" (*World Order* 147) and "the preliminary steps" (*God Passes By* 329) during the Heroic Age of our Faith in anticipation of the future Administrative Order.

These are his exact words:

> In the Tablets of Bahá'u'lláh where the institutions of the International and Local Houses of Justice are specifically designated and formally established; in the institution of

the Hands of the Cause of God which first Bahá'u'lláh and then 'Abdu'l-Bahá brought into being; in the institution of both local and national Assemblies which in their embryonic stage were already functioning in the days preceding 'Abdu'l-Bahá's ascension; in the authority with which the Author of our Faith and the Center of His Covenant have in their Tablets chosen to confer upon them; in the institution of the Local Fund which operated according to 'Abdu'l-Bahá's specific injunctions addressed to certain Assemblies in Persia; in the verses of the Kitáb-i-Aqdas the implications of which clearly anticipate the institution of the Guardianship; in the explanation which 'Abdu'l-Bahá, in one of His Tablets, has given to, and the emphasis He has placed upon, the hereditary principle and the law of primogeniture as having been upheld by the Prophets of the past—in these we can discern the faint glimmerings and discover the earliest intimation of the nature and working of the Administrative Order which the Will of 'Abdu'l-Bahá was at a later time destined to proclaim and formally establish. (*World Order* 147)

The second passage is as follows:

It should be borne in mind... that the preliminary steps aiming at the disclosure of the scope and working of this Administrative Order, which was now to be formally established after 'Abdu'l-Bahá's passing, had already been taken by Him, and even by Bahá'u'lláh in the years preceding His ascension. The appointment by Him of certain outstanding believers in Persia as "Hands of the Cause"; the initiation of local Assemblies and boards of consultation by 'Abdu'l-Bahá in leading Bahá'í centers in both the East and the West; the formation of the Bahá'í Temple Unity in the United States of America; the establishment of local funds for the promotion of Bahá'í activities; the purchase of property dedicated to the Faith and its future institutions; the founding of publishing societies for the dissemination of Bahá'í literature; the erection of the first Mashriqu'l-Adhkár of the Bahá'í world; the construction of the Báb's mausoleum on Mt. Carmel; the institution of hostels for the accommodation of itinerant teachers and pilgrims—these may be regarded as the precursors of the institutions which, immediately after the closing of the Heroic Age of the Faith, were to be permanently and systematically established throughout the Bahá'í world. (*God Passes By* 329–30)

As you see, the second extract has a few repetitious items, but it also has many additional elements. To illustrate the rudimentary manner in which these boards of consultation operated when they were first formed during the ministry of 'Abdu'l-Bahá, I will give you one instance.

The Local Spiritual Assembly of Ṭihrán, which was formed in 1897, was the first in the whole country. As the members did not have any by-laws, they decided to have a seal, which was divided into nine slices. When the Assembly met, and after a decision was taken, the Secretary had to draft the letter at the meeting and read it to the members. Each member kept one slice of the seal with him, and when the letter was approved he would part with his slice so that the nine slices could be combined in a special frame to make it possible for the seal to be affixed on the approved letter. At the end of the meeting, obviously, each member went home with his own slice in his pocket.

Likewise, the first Local Assembly of the United States was established in Chicago, and having assumed the title of the Chicago House of Justice it was so addressed by 'Abdu'l-Bahá Himself (*World Order* 6). However, later He advised that the temporary appellation of Local Spiritual Assembly was more appropriate.

Under the guidance of the Guardian, the phoenix of the system of Bahá'í Administration rose from the ashes of these precursors and forerunners of the institutions of our Faith. Even after the dissemination of the Will and Testament of 'Abdu'l-Bahá, it took Shoghi Effendi many months, and in some cases several years, to fully explain to the friends in countries in the East and West where a sufficient number of Bahá'ís resided the essential requirements for forming their Local Spiritual Assemblies on a sound constitutional basis, to direct them subsequently on how to elect their delegates on a proportionate basis in order to hold their National Conventions, and to guide them finally in forming their National Spiritual Assemblies, which were to serve as pillars supporting the dome—the dome being the long-anticipated Universal House of Justice.

As I have already indicated, Shoghi Effendi referred in his writings to the administrative structure that he was guiding the Bahá'ís to erect as the "Bahá'í Administration". He used an equivalent term in his Persian letters to the friends in the East. It was only after 13 years that he used the rightful title, namely, the Bahá'í Administrative Order, to refer to the administrative system that had just begun to operate in accordance with the guidelines he had provided.

In the early years of Shoghi Effendi's Guardianship, the administrative structure being erected and becoming visible was clearly modest in character and scope, and, therefore, the simple descriptive title "Bahá'í Administration" suited it very well. However, beyond this, it should be borne in mind that Shoghi Effendi was essentially a modest person. For example, when he was translating the text of the Will and Testament of 'Abdu'l-Bahá immediately after the Master's passing, he used the lower case for both "guardian" and "branch" when they referred to him. However, 13 years later, when he was quoting from 'Abdu'l-Bahá Will in the "Dispensation", he capitalized both "Guardian" and "Branch". He could well have sensed that his

111

station as Guardian would have been by then more readily understood and accepted.

In view of its importance, I would like to quote again the celebrated passage in the Kitáb-i-Aqdas which formally announces the emergence of Bahá'u'lláh's new World Order: "The world's equilibrium hath been upset through the vibrating influence of this most great, this new World Order. Mankind's ordered life hath been revolutionized through the agency of this unique, this wondrous system—the like of which mortal eyes have never witnessed" (¶181).

Until that day in 1934 when Shoghi Effendi produced his translation of this key verse in Bahá'u'lláh's Mother Book, the generality of the Bahá'ís understood it to mean that the order of the verses of the Aqdas followed a unique arrangement, different from that of the Bayán or other holy books of former dispensations. There is a verse in the Bayán which also refers to the Order of Bahá'u'lláh. This corresponding verse was also understood along the same lines; in other words, the Aqdas, unlike the Bayán, would have a unique format of its own.

When I was on pilgrimage in 1957, Shoghi Effendi on one occasion quoted this verse of the Aqdas. As there was a pause after his recital of the verse, I took the liberty of mentioning to him how scholars of the Faith in Iran had totally misunderstood the meaning of this verse and that in the classes that I had attended this misconception was taught to the students. And I added, "Where would the Bahá'í world be without the beloved Guardian?" At this remark, Shoghi Effendi smiled and he said, "Nicolas understood, but the friends did not". Mr Nicolas was a French Orientalist, and although he was not a Bábí nor a Bahá'í, he was an admirer of the Báb and translated both the Persian and Arabic Bayáns into French.

When one reads the letters of the Guardian in both English and Persian during his ministry, it is not difficult to see that he had two main objectives in mind. As to the first objective, it was clear to him that the Universal House of Justice, which was the last unit of the edifice of the Administrative Order, was like the dome, the crown, the apex of the structure, and he clearly stated this in his writings. This dome could not hang in the air without the support of columns. These columns were none other than the National Spiritual Assemblies. Even nine of them would have been adequate, but indeed the more of them the better. These National Assemblies, however, had to rest on the firm foundation of Local Spiritual Assemblies, which themselves had to be formed on a sound and solid basis. As early as March 1923 he wrote the following: "With these Assemblies, local as well as national, harmoniously, vigorously, and efficiently functioning throughout the Bahá'í world, the only means for the establishment of the Supreme House of Justice will have been secured" (*Bahá'í Administration* 41).

The second objective which he focused upon was to use these administrative institutions to promote the teaching work unitedly and systematically. There was no charter for this worldwide activity more appropriate than the Master's Tablets of the Divine Plan. Therefore, not only did he want to see each National Assembly engaged in carrying out the objectives of a teaching and consolidation plan within its jurisdiction, but his ultimate goal was to build bridges among these National Assemblies.

A slight diversion from the main theme of this discussion would be helpful. When the British Bahá'ís completed their Six Year Plan in 1951 Shoghi Effendi advised the British National Assembly that he wanted it to immediately launch a Two Year Plan, aimed primarily at the settlement of pioneers and the promotion of the teaching work in both East and West Africa. He also called on the National Spiritual Assemblies of the United States, Persia, Egypt, and India to collaborate with the British National Assembly on this project. In his messages inaugurating this two-year phase of inter-National Spiritual Assembly collaboration, he anticipated a subsequent stage of collaborative efforts among *all* National Spiritual Assemblies of the world. This was clearly an anticipation of the launching of his Ten Year

Crusade. He went on to state that such undertakings would be a prelude to future teaching and pioneering enterprises embarked upon and conducted by the Universal House of Justice.

Commenting on its election, the Universal House of Justice wrote on 9 March 1965 in one of its early letters as follows:

> The Guardian had given the Bahá'í world explicit and detailed plans covering the period until Riḍván 1963, the end of the Ten Year Crusade. From that point onward, unless the Faith were to be endangered, further divine guidance was essential. This was the second pressing reason for the calling of the election of the Universal House of Justice. The rightness of the time was further confirmed by references in Shoghi Effendi's letters to the Ten Year Crusade's being followed by other plans under the direction of the Universal House of Justice. One such reference is the following passage from a letter addressed to the National Spiritual Assembly of the British Isles on 25ᵗʰ February 1951, concerning its Two Year Plan which immediately preceded the Ten Year Crusade: "On the success of this enterprise, unprecedented in its scope, unique in its character and immense in its spiritual potentialities, must depend the initiation, at a later period in the Formative Age of the Faith, of undertakings embracing within their range all National Assemblies functioning throughout the Bahá'í world—undertakings constituting in themselves a prelude to the launching of worldwide enterprises destined to be embarked upon, in future epochs of that same Age, by the Universal House of Justice, that will symbolize the unity and co-ordinate and unify the activities of these National Assemblies. (*Messages from the Universal House of Justice* ¶23.6)

The Guardian sent a similar message to the National Assembly of the United States. I was in Ṭihrán at the time and was on the National Assembly of Iran. I remember the consternation this message produced. It was not because the election of the Universal House of Justice was drawing so near but because it was that body, which was essentially a legislative body, and not the Guardian, who was always associated with teaching plans, that was to launch and direct the future teaching work.

When the Hands of the Cause throughout the world, who had just been in October 1957 invested by the Guardian with the title of "Chief Stewards of Bahá'u'lláh's embryonic World Commonwealth", convened in the Holy Land in November of that year after his passing, they soon realized that there was no choice for the Bahá'í world but to move on and continue to operate under the guidance of the goals of the Ten Year Crusade until 1963, when the Universal House of Justice would be formed. Towards the end of his life, Shoghi Effendi wrote on more than one occasion that on such a day the prophecy of Daniel about the 1,335 days would be fulfilled, as 'Abdu'l-Bahá had predicted: "on that day will the faithful rejoice with exceeding gladness" (*Messages to the Bahá'í World* 44).

As I have already indicated, the long-range objective of the Faith of Bahá'u'lláh is the Most Great Peace, which will give birth to a Bahá'í civilization the like of which mankind has never witnessed. The Administrative Order, preceded by the Bahá'í Administration, is but a preliminary stage in this process. This Administrative Order has been described by Shoghi Effendi as the embryonic stage which will lead to the emergence of the World Order of Bahá'u'lláh. This in turn will develop into the Bahá'í World Commonwealth, which will produce the Most Great Peace and subsequently the Bahá'í World Civilization. To sum it up, the stages through which this process will develop are the Bahá'í Administration, the Bahá'í Administrative Order, Bahá'u'lláh's new World Order—signalizing the advent of the Golden Age of His Faith, the Bahá'í World Commonwealth, the

Most Great Peace, and, finally, the birth of the promised new civilization.

On more than one occasion, Shoghi Effendi has explained that there is a difference between the Administrative Order and the World Order. The former, as I just stated, is the embryonic stage of the latter, the latter being the new World Order yet to be born. The lack of pleasing proportions in the various parts of an embryo, in the eyes of an ignorant viewer, would give the impression of ugliness, incongruity, and imperfection. However, in the eyes of a wise and intelligent observer, the lack of apparent coherence is only a necessary stage in the development not of a seemingly monstrous creature but of a highly sensitive, continuously evolving, and organically ripening embryo. When the decreed moment arrives and it is duly born, it will be a delight to all eyes—a charming baby with its bewitching smile.

The reason why I am drawing this parallel is to show the difference between the two outlooks: one is studied, well-informed, and wisely concluded, the other is unstudied, rash, and impulsive. I am sorry to say that we hear many remarks of the second category from Bahá'ís around us who are well meaning but unfortunately have failed to understand the processes which are at work. When they see in the operation of our embryonic institutions some awkwardness and clumsiness, they impatiently voice their criticism, which, though not viciously intended, can quite often arouse discontent and even be destructive.

Because of the emphasis which 'Abdu'l-Bahá placed on the spiritual principles which should govern and distinguish our Bahá'í community life, many Bahá'ís in the West had the false conception that organization was foreign to the aims and purposes of the Bahá'í Religion.

Indeed, towards the end of the life of 'Abdu'l-Bahá, a pilgrim's note attributed to Him was circulated among the friends in the United States to the effect that the Bahá'í Faith had no organization. When 'Abdu'l-Bahá was asked whether such a statement was true, He categorically denied it. Unfortunately, this pilgrim's note remained alive, and when Shoghi Effendi began calling on the friends to lay the foundations of their Local Assemblies and prepare for the establishment of their National Assemblies, he found that he once again had to explicitly state that the pilgrim's note attributed to 'Abdu'l-Bahá was baseless.

In February 1929 he had to write the following to the friends in the United States and Canada:

I am at a loss to explain that strange mentality that inclines to uphold as the sole criterion of the truth of the Bahá'í Teachings what is admittedly only an obscure and unauthenticated translation of an oral statement made by 'Abdu'l-Bahá, in defiance and total disregard of the available text of all of His universally recognized writings. I truly deplore the unfortunate distortions that have resulted in days past from the incapacity of the interpreter to grasp the meaning of 'Abdu'l-Bahá, and from his incompetence to render adequately such truths as have been revealed to him by the Master's statements. Much of the confusion that has obscured the understanding of the believers should be attributed to this double error involved in the inexact rendering of an only partially understood statement. Not infrequently has the interpreter even failed to convey the exact purport of the inquirer's specific questions, and, by his deficiency of understanding and expression in conveying the answer of 'Abdu'l-Bahá, has been responsible for reports wholly at variance with the true spirit and purpose of the Cause. (*World Order* 4–5).

He wrote the following on the same date:

Who, I may ask, when viewing the international character of the Cause, its far-flung ramifications, the increasing complexity of its affairs, the diversity of its adherents, and the state of confusion that assails on every side the infant

Faith of God, can for a moment question the necessity of some sort of administrative machinery that will insure, amid the storm and stress of a struggling civilization, the unity of the Faith, the preservation of its identity, and the protection of its interests? To repudiate the validity of the assemblies of the elected ministers of the Faith of Bahá'u'lláh would be to reject those countless Tablets of Bahá'u'lláh and 'Abdu'l-Bahá wherein They have extolled the station of the "trustees of the Merciful," enumerated their privileges and duties, emphasized the glory of their mission, revealed the immensity of their task, and warned them of the attacks they must needs expect from the unwisdom of their friends as well as from the malice of their enemies. (*World Order* 9–10)

Thanks to these explanations, the attacks levelled against the Guardian by such people as Ruth White and Ahmad Sohrab were overcome. The clarity of Shoghi Effendi's elucidations and the steadfast and loyal adherence of the friends to the provisions of the Will and Testament of 'Abdu'l-Bahá put an end to this controversy.

So much for the form of the Administrative Order and its necessity and its indispensability. If the form, however, is not quickened with the spirit, it remains a dead form. This is why Shoghi Effendi, from the very outset of his clarifications of the principles underlying the Administration of the Faith, kept reminding the friends of the absolute necessity to develop and nurture the spirit which should always be at its very core and illumine the path which the institutions are called upon to follow.

From his pen flowed such exhortations as the following three excerpts. In March 1923 he wrote,

But let us be on our guard—so the Master continually reminds us from His Station on high—lest too much concern in that which is secondary in importance, and too long a preoccupation with the details of our affairs and activities, make us neglectful of the most essential, the most urgent of all our obligations, namely, to bury our cares and teach the Cause, delivering far and wide this Message of Salvation to a sorely-stricken world. (*Bahá'í Administration* 42)

In February 1929 he wrote,

And now, it behoves us to reflect on the animating purpose and the primary functions of these divinely-established institutions, the sacred character and the universal efficacy of which can be demonstrated only by the spirit they diffuse and the work they actually achieve. I need not dwell upon what I have already reiterated and emphasized that the administration of the Cause is to be conceived as an instrument and not a substitute for the Faith of Bahá'u'lláh, that it should be regarded as a channel through which His promised blessings may flow, that it should guard against such rigidity as would clog and fetter the liberating forces released by His Revelation... It is surely for those to whose hands so priceless a heritage has been committed to prayerfully watch lest the tool should supersede the Faith itself, lest undue concern for the minute details arising from the administration of the Cause obscure the vision of its promoters, lest partiality, ambition, and worldliness tend in the course of time to becloud the radiance, stain the purity, and impair the effectiveness of the Faith of Bahá'u'lláh. (*World Order* 9–10)

We should note the evils we are to avoid as servants of this Faith, namely, partiality, ambition, and worldliness.

In December 1935, writing to an individual believer, he wrote the following:

The Bahá'í Faith, like all other Divine religions, is thus fundamentally mystic in character. Its chief goal is the development of the individual and society, through the acquisition of spiritual virtues and powers. It is the soul of man that has first to be fed. And this spiritual nourishment prayer can best provide. Laws and institutions, as viewed by Bahá'u'lláh, can become really effective only when our inner spiritual life has been perfected and transformed. Otherwise religion will degenerate into a mere organization, and become a dead thing. (*Messages from the Universal House of Justice* ¶397.2c)

We should realize how through lack of effort on our part in transforming our inner spiritual lives we could kill the spirit of the Faith and cause the institutions of the Administrative Order to become mere lifeless things.

We should also remember that statements such as these made by the beloved Guardian are in full harmony with what Bahá'u'lláh states in the Kitáb-i-Aqdas, namely, that members of Houses of Justice, when meeting, "should consider themselves as entering the Court of the presence of God, the Exalted, the Most High, and as beholding Him Who is the Unseen". Bahá'u'lláh further calls on them to "regard themselves as the guardians appointed of God for all that dwell on earth" and "to have regard for the interests of the servants of God, for His sake, even as they regard their own interests, and to choose that which is meet and seemly. Thus hath the Lord your God commanded you. Beware lest ye put away that which is clearly revealed in His Tablet. Fear God, O ye that perceive" (¶30). In these immortal verses of the Aqdas, Bahá'u'lláh is urging members of Spiritual Assemblies not only to be deeply spiritual but also to be selfless, altruistic, and universally minded.

Shoghi Effendi went on to explain, "Let us also bear in mind that the keynote of the Cause of God is not dictatorial authority but humble fellowship, not arbitrary power, but the spirit of frank and loving consultation" (*Bahá'í Administration* 63). The spiritual obligations of the elected representatives of the Faith have been set forth by Shoghi Effendi in the following words:

Their function is not to dictate, but to consult, and consult not only among themselves, but as much as possible with the friends whom they represent. They must regard themselves in no other light but that of chosen instruments for a more efficient and dignified presentation of the Cause of God. They should never be led to suppose that they are the central ornaments of the body of the Cause, intrinsically superior to others in capacity or merit, and sole promoters of its teachings and principles. They should approach their task with extreme humility, and endeavor, by their open-mindedness, their high sense of justice and duty, their candor, their modesty, their entire devotion to the welfare and interests of the friends, the Cause, and humanity, to win, not only the confidence and the genuine support and respect of those whom they serve, but also their esteem and real affection. They must, at all times, avoid the spirit of exclusiveness, the atmosphere of secrecy, free themselves from a domineering attitude, and banish all forms of prejudice and passion from their deliberations. They should, within the limits of wise discretion, take the friends into their confidence, acquaint them with their plans, share with them their problems and anxieties, and seek their advice and counsel. And, when they are called upon to arrive at a certain decision, they should, after dispassionate, anxious and cordial consultation, turn to God in prayer, and with earnestness and conviction and courage record their vote and abide by the voice of the majority... (*Bahá'í Administration* 64).

As you see from the above, both spirit and form are important, and the more important is the spirit of love, humility, and dedication which must inform the consultations and actions of all elected institutions of the Faith.

There is no doubt that this spirit should also be the motivating force that inspires those who are privileged to serve as appointed promoters and protectors of the Cause, such as Counsellors, Auxiliary Board members, and assistants.

When Shoghi Effendi was asked to give the qualifications of a true believer, for the benefit of Spiritual Assemblies which were considering membership of applicants to the Bahá'í community, one of the essential qualifications he stipulated was "close association with the spirit as well as the form of the present day Bahá'í administration" (*Bahá'í Administration* 90). This is one of the vital administrative principles of our Faith. The individual is an organic part of his community. He cannot, and must not, dissociate himself from community activities. One of the distinctions of our Faith is the essential contribution of the individual to the life of the community, which in turn, as it develops, exerts its healthy influence on the individual and promotes his spiritual advancement. In the Aqdas Bahá'u'lláh tells us that individuals are like constituent elements and members of the human body. This means that the well-being of the part is the well-being of all. The injury of the part is the injury of all. Furthermore, the community can serve as a laboratory in which the individual translates the ideals and principles of the Faith which he has imbibed into concrete and constructive action. Participation in the work of the community thus becomes a learning process for better understanding how the theory taught by the Faith can be realized in service in the field. All this means that, as devoted Bahá'ís, we should avoid two extremes: (1) Adherence to the laws and ordinances of the Faith as applicable to the individual, with the exception of association with the community, and (2) Total involvement in community activities, with the exception of following the Bahá'í way of life, which is binding on the individual.

The final part of this section is about the rulers and the learned—who they are, how they complement each other, and what the spiritual ties are that bind them together and to the rest of the community. In a letter dated 23 April 1972, the Universal House of Justice, addressing this question, wrote,

> In the Kitáb-i-'Ahd (the Book of His Covenant) Bahá'u'lláh wrote "Blessed are the rulers and the learned among the people of Bahá," and referring to this very passage the beloved Guardian wrote on 4 November 1931: "In this holy cycle the 'learned' are, on the one hand, the Hands of the Cause of God, and, on the other, the teachers and diffusers of His teachings who do not rank as Hands, but who have attained an eminent position in the teaching work. As to the 'rulers' they refer to the members of the Local, National and International Houses of Justice. The duties of each of these souls will be determined in the future." (*Messages from the Universal House of Justice* ¶111.3)

After quoting the Guardian, the Universal House of Justice has commented as follows:

> The Hands of the Cause of God, the Counsellors and the members of the Auxiliary Boards fall within the definition of the "learned" given by the beloved Guardian... When, following the passing of Shoghi Effendi, the Universal House of Justice decided that it could not legislate to make possible the appointment of further Hands of the Cause, it became necessary for it to create a new institution, appointed by itself, to extend into the future the functions of protection and propagation vested in the Hands of the Cause and, with that in view, so to develop the Institution

of the Hands that it could nurture the new institution and function in close collaboration with it as long as possible. It was also vital so to arrange matters as to make the most effective use of the unique services of the Hands themselves..." (*Messages from the Universal House of Justice* ¶111.4–6)

In the same letter, the Universal House of Justice quotes from a letter of Shoghi Effendi:

In a letter written on 14 March 1927 to the Spiritual Assembly of the Bahá'ís of Istanbul, the Guardian's Secretary explained, on his behalf, the principle in the Cause of action by majority vote. He pointed out how, in the past, it was certain individuals who "accounted themselves as superior in knowledge and elevated in position" who caused division, and that it was those "who pretended to be the most distinguished of all" who "always proved themselves to be the source of contention." "But praise be to God," he continued, "that the Pen of Glory has done away with the unyielding and dictatorial views of the learned and the wise, dismissed the assertions of individuals as an authoritative criterion, even though they were recognized as the most accomplished and learned among men and ordained that all matters be referred to authorized centres and specified Assemblies. Even so, no Assembly has been invested with the absolute authority to deal with such general matters as affect the interests of nations. Nay rather, He has brought all the assemblies together under the shadow of one House of Justice, one divinely appointed Centre, so that there would be only one Centre and all the rest integrated into a single body, revolving around one expressly designated Pivot, thus making them all proof against schism and division. (*Messages from the Universal House of Justice* ¶111.12)

After quoting this passage from Shoghi Effendi's letter, the Universal House of Justice draws the following conclusions:

Having permanently excluded the evils admittedly inherent in the institutions of the "learned" in past dispensations, Bahá'u'lláh has nevertheless embodied in His Administrative Order the beneficent elements which exist in such institutions, elements which are of fundamental value for the progress of the Cause, as can be gauged from even a cursory reading of the Guardian's message of 4 June 1957.

The existence of institutions of such exalted rank, comprising individuals who play such a vital role, who yet have no legislative, administrative or judicial authority, and are entirely devoid of priestly functions or the right to make authoritative interpretations, is a feature of Bahá'í administration unparalleled in the religions of the past. The newness and uniqueness of this concept make it difficult to grasp; only as the Bahá'í Community grows and the believers are increasingly able to contemplate its administrative structure uninfluenced by concepts from past ages, will the vital interdependence of the "rulers" and "learned" in the Faith be properly understood, and the inestimable value of their interaction be fully recognized. (*Messages from the Universal House of Justice* ¶111.13–14)

Some six years later, a question related to this theme was asked by one of the believers, and this needed further clarification of the issues involved. On 27 March 1978 the Department of the Secretariat, writing on behalf of the Universal House of Justice, gave the following elucidation:

A Board of Counsellors has the particular responsibility of caring for the protection and propagation of the Faith throughout a continental zone which contains a number of national Bahá'í communities. In performing these tasks it neither directs nor instructs the Spiritual Assemblies or individual believers, but it has the necessary rank to enable it to ensure that it is kept properly informed and that the Spiritual Assemblies give due consideration to its advice and recommendations. However, the essence of the relationships between Bahá'í institutions is loving consultation and a common desire to serve the Cause of God rather than a matter of rank or station.

It is clear from the Writings of Bahá'u'lláh, as well as from those of 'Abdu'l-Bahá and the interpretations of the Guardian, that the proper functioning of human society requires the preservation of ranks and classes within its membership. The friends should recognize this without envy or jealousy, and those who occupy ranks should never exploit their position or regard themselves as being superior to others.

About this Bahá'u'lláh has written:

> And amongst the realms of unity is the unity of rank and station. It redoundeth to the exaltation of the Cause, glorifying it among all peoples. Ever since the seeking of preference and distinction came into play, the world hath been laid waste. It hath become desolate. Those who have quaffed from the ocean of divine utterance and fixed their gaze upon the Realm of Glory should regard themselves as being on the same level as the others and in the same station. Were this matter to be definitely established and conclusively demonstrated through the power and might of God, the world would become as the Abhá Paradise.

Indeed, man is noble, inasmuch as each one is a repository of the sign of God. Nevertheless, to regard oneself as superior in knowledge, learning or virtue, or to exalt oneself or seek preference, is a grievous transgression. Great is the blessedness of those who are adorned with the ornament of this unity and have been graciously confirmed by God. (*Messages from the Universal House of Justice* ¶206.2–3b)

Thus ends the quotation from Bahá'u'lláh.
The letter of the House of Justice goes on to say,

Courtesy, reverence, dignity, respect for the rank and achievements of others are virtues which contribute to the harmony and well-being of every community, but pride and self-aggrandizement are among the most deadly of sins...

The House of Justice hopes that all the friends will remember that the ultimate aim in life of every soul should be to attain spiritual excellence—to win the good pleasure of God. The true spiritual station of any soul is known only to God. It is quite a different thing from the ranks and stations that men and women occupy in the various sectors of society. Whoever has his eyes fixed on the goal of attaining the good pleasure of God will accept with joy and radiant acquiescence whatever work or station is assigned to him in the Cause of God, and will rejoice to serve Him under all conditions. (*Messages from the Universal House of Justice* ¶206.4–5)

The House of Justice is giving us in this letter a clarification which is unique in organizational philosophy. The first point is the House's acceptance of the policy generally practiced in any form of secular or religious administration, namely, that without positions and ranks no organization can efficiently function. After this assertion, and based on a remarkable text by Bahá'u'lláh Himself, the House of Justice exhorts the Bahá'í rulers and the Bahá'í learned by saying in effect the following: Be not concerned that your positions will not be preserved or respected by those who are beneath you in rank or achievement, but let not this outward consideration give you pride, and let it not deceive you into thinking that you are morally and essentially better than them. True ranks are known solely to God and will be revealed to men's eyes only in the next world. Therefore do not act arrogantly towards others and do not exalt yourself over them by virtue of a temporary privilege given to you in this world. (These are of course only my own words summing up the House of Justice's exhortation.) In one of His Tablets Bahá'u'lláh says that the more we fear God in our lives with genuine humility the nearer will we be to God in this world and the next.

No other organizational system I know of, whether religious or secular, has such a fundamentally moral and spiritual concept incorporated in its structure. It is this attitude which gives spirit to our community and administrative activities. It is indeed one of the distinctive features of the Bahá'í Administrative Order, which is not an earthly man-made organization but is essentially a divinely conceived and providentially sustained system, destined to embrace, unify, and uplift humanity.

Questions related:

Q. A non-Bahá'í friend of mine said he thought it was not fair that only "famous" Bahá'ís would be elected and that their visibility in the community was perhaps a hidden form of campaigning. What do you think?

A. The use of the word "famous" in this context is both inaccurate and inappropriate. In one of His Tablets 'Abdu'l-Bahá refers to the elected members as souls of good repute whose fair name has spread like the fragrance of musk among the people. Some Bahá'ís may be famous but not have a good reputation. In Bahá'í elections you should look for the qualities that members of the community are known to possess. These qualities are unquestioned loyalty, selfless devotion, a well-trained mind, recognized ability, and mature experience (*Bahá'í Administration* 88). We should also remember that, as electors, we should engage in the act of election in a prayerful attitude and supplicate the Blessed Beauty to grant us His guidance.

Q. Shoghi Effendi writes about "Divine Economy". Could you explain what it means?

A. If you look up the word "economy" in reliable dictionaries you will see that one of its meanings is a system of organization. I think in the reference you have mentioned we should understand Shoghi Effendi's use of this term as applying to the Administrative Order.

Q. One of the prime requisites of the Assembly members, according to 'Abdu'l-Bahá is, "purity of motive", and He mentions this quality before all other virtues. What is your understanding of "purity of motive"?

A. In the Persian Hidden Words Bahá'u'lláh refers to "pure and goodly deeds" and adds that "ere long the assayers of mankind shall, in the Holy Presence of the Adored One, accept naught but absolute virtue and deeds of stainless purity" (Hidden Words, Persian, no. 69). My understanding of purity of motive is deeds of service that are performed, either in the work of the administration or in the teaching field, solely for the sake of winning the good pleasure of the Blessed Beauty. I think purity of motive requires us to set aside all other considerations, whether they are earthly things outside the pale of the Faith or spiritual rewards within the Cause, or as it is sometimes expressed, "within the precincts" of God's Holy Faith. I think this is what is meant by the following sentence in the Tablet of Visitation of 'Abdu'l-Bahá: "Help me to be selfless at the heavenly entrance of Thy gate, and aid me to be detached from all things within Thy holy precincts". If we want to have pure motives we should be satisfied in our confidence that He sees us and that He knows us. Our one and only motivation in Bahá'í activities and in obedience to His commands should be that our humble offering of unworthy services and deeds may be acceptable in His sight.

Q. Where in the text of the Kitáb-i-Aqdas does Bahá'u'lláh anticipate the institution of the Guardianship?

A. Shoghi Effendi wrote in February 1929, "By leaving certain matters unspecified and unregulated in His Book of Laws, Bahá'u'lláh seems to have deliberately left a gap in the general scheme of Bahá'í Dispensation, which the unequivocal provisions of the Master's Will has filled" (*World Order* 4). One of the "unspecified" matters is the question of who will be the recipient of Ḥuqúqu'lláh after Bahá'u'lláh. The obvious conclusion was, of course, drawn that whoever or whatever institution was the Successor of Bahá'u'lláh and occupied the position of Headship of the Faith would be the recipient. Thus,

Ḥuqúq was paid first to 'Abdu'l-Bahá and then subsequently, in accordance with His Will, to the Guardian. This is one way the institution of the Guardianship was anticipated, and I have mentioned this point already. Another place in the Aqdas which could well be another intimation of the Guardianship is the verse in which Bahá'u'lláh says that "whatsoever ye understand not in the Book" should be referred to the Branch grown out "from this mighty Stock" (¶174). It is in this verse that the function of authorized interpretation has been given to the Branch, and it seems to be that this is the second verse where the position of the Guardian, as authorized interpreter, has been anticipated.

BIBLIOGRAPHY

'Abdu'l-Bahá. *Selections from the Writings of 'Abdu'l-Bahá.*
Compiled by the Research Department of the Universal House
of Justice. Translated by a Committee at the Bahá'í World
Centre and Marzieh Gail. Wilmette: Bahá'í Publishing Trust,
1997.
— *Some Answered Questions.* Collected and translated from the
Persian by Laura Clifford Barney. Wilmette: Bahá'í Publishing
Trust, 1984.
— *Will and Testament of 'Abdu'l-Bahá.* Wilmette: Bahá'í Publishing
Trust, 1944.
The Báb. *Selections from the Writings of the Báb.* Compiled by the
Research Department of the Universal House of Justice.
Translated by Habib Taherzadeh et al. Haifa: Bahá'í World
Centre, 1976.
Bahá'í Prayers. London: Bahá'í Publishing Trust, 1975.
The Bahá'í World: An International Record, 1954–1963. Vol. XIII.
Prepared under the supervision of the Universal House of
Justice. Haifa: The Universal House of Justice, 1970.
Bahá'u'lláh. *Epistle to the Son of the Wolf.* Translated by Shoghi
Effendi. Wilmette: Bahá'í Publishing Trust, 1988.
— *Gleanings from the Writings of Bahá'u'lláh.* Translated by Shoghi
Effendi. Wilmette: Bahá'í Publishing Trust, 1983.
— *The Hidden Words.* Translated by Shoghi Effendi. Wilmette:
Bahá'í Publishing Trust, 1985.
— *The Kitáb-i-Aqdas: The Most Holy Book.* Wilmette: Bahá'í
Publishing Trust, 1993.
— *Tablets of Bahá'u'lláh revealed after the Kitáb-i-Aqdas.* Compiled
by the Research Department of the Universal House of Justice.
Translated by Habib Taherzadeh et al. Wilmette: Bahá'í
Publishing Trust, 1988.
Lights of Guidance: A Bahá'í Reference File. Compiled by Helen
Bassett Hornby. New Delhi: Bahá'í Publishing Trust, 1994.
*The Right of God/Ḥuqúqu'lláh: Extracts from the Writings of
Bahá'u'lláh, 'Abdu'l-Bahá, Shoghi Effendi and the Universal
House of Justice, with Supplement.* Compiled by the Research

Department of the Universal House of Justice. Thornhill: Bahá'í Community of Canada, 1999.

Rabbani, Rúḥíyyih. *The Priceless Pearl.* London: Bahá'í Publishing Trust, 1969.

Shoghi Effendi. *The Advent of Divine Justice.* Wilmette: Bahá'í Publishing Trust, 1990.

— *Bahá'í Administration.* Wilmette: Bahá'í Publishing Trust, 1960.

— *Call to the Nations.* Haifa: Bahá'í World Centre, 1977.

— *Citadel of Faith: Messages to America, 1947–1957.* Wilmette: Bahá'í Publishing Trust, 1965.

— *This Decisive Hour: Messages from Shoghi Effendi to the North American Bahá'ís, 1932–1946.* Wilmette: Bahá'í Publishing Trust, 2002.

— *God Passes By.* Wilmette: Bahá'í Publishing Trust, 1970.

— *Messages to the Bahá'í World, 1950–1957.* Wilmette: Bahá'í Publishing Trust, 1971.

— *The Promised Day Is Come.* Wilmette: Bahá'í Publishing Trust, 1996.

— *The World Order of Bahá'u'lláh.* Wilmette: Bahá'í Publishing Trust, 1955.

The Universal House of Justice. *The Constitution of the Universal House of Justice.* Haifa: Bahá'í World Centre, 1972.

— *Messages from the Universal House of Justice, 1963–1986: The Third Epoch of the Formative Age.* Compiled by Geoffry W. Marks. Wilmette: Bahá'í Publishing Trust, 1996.

— *A Wider Horizon: Selected Messages of the Universal House of Justice, 1983–1992.* Compiled by Paul Lample. Riviera Beach: Palabra Publications, 1992.